SAARC

SAARC

SAPTA to SAFTA

Anshuman Gupta

MAULANA ABUL KALAM AZAD INSTITUTE OF ASIAN STUDIES, KOLKATA

SHIPRA

Published on behalf of Maulana Abul Kalam Azad Institute of Asian Studies, Kolkata. The views expressed are of the author and don't represent the viewpoint of the Institute as such.

ISBN 81-7541-107-4

First Published in India in 2002

SAARC: SAPTA to SAFTA

Published by:
SHIPRA PUBLICATIONS
115A, Shakarpur, Vikas Marg
Delhi-110092, INDIA
Phone: 2458662, 2200954 Fax: 91-11-2423078
Email: siprapubs@satyam.net.in

Laser Typeset by:
Kumar DTP Systems
Delhi-110091

Printed at:
Choudhary Offset Process
Delhi-110051

Preface

The South Asian region, which prides itself for being the prime centre of learning in the remote past and one of the early cradles of civilization, is at present reeling under dire poverty and deprivation. All human development indicators, including literacy, infant mortality and population growth rate, per capita income, etc., are showing dismal performance though in varying degree. The average per capita income in the countries of the region is below $600, with Sri Lanka having the highest. Almost half of the population of the region is below poverty line. This poor performance on all counts is linked with low economic growth rate persistently recorded by the countries of the region. This hardly conforms to the past image of the Indian sub-continent as the 'golden bird' owing to its affluence and prosperity. Most of the countries of the region have been engaged in the zero-sum territorial disputes at the expense of non-zero sum economic cooperation, which has been an important factor responsible for the underdevelopment of the region. This is in marked contrast with majority of countries in the world, especially developed ones, which have substantially increased their economic welfare through regional trading blocs by creating trade among themselves.

Albeit late, the countries of the region also recognized the importance of regional cooperation and set up the South Asian Association for Regional Cooperation (SAARC) in 1985. An attempt was made to strengthen economic cooperation through forging SAARC Preferential Trading Arrangement (SAPTA) in 1995. It was planned to convert it into a full-fledged Economic Union (EU) by 2020, through the successive stages of South Asian Free Trade Area (SAFTA) by 2010 and Customs Union by 2015. Three rounds of negotiations have already taken place under SAPTA, the last one being in 1998. The fourth one is in progress. It is, however, inordinately delayed mainly on account of increased distrust between India and Pakistan over the territorial dispute of Kashmir in the wake of the Kargil misadventure and the end of democratic rule in Pakistan. The high expectations of the regional economic integration scheme in South Asia thus remain at stake as before. The grim scenario of regional economic cooperation among South Asian countries under SAPTA and the chequered course of upgrading it through progress towards the cherished goal of setting up the South Asian Free Trade Area (SAFTA) calls for a serious investigation. The present work is a modest attempt in this direction.

I am indebted to Maulana Abul Kalam Azad Institute of Asian Studies and its Director Prof. Mahavir Singh for providing me an opportunity to work on this topic. I am also thankful to Prof. Devendra Kaushik, Chairman of Executive Council of the Institute for animated discussions which have greatly helped me in evaluating the unfolding regional cooperation in the South Asian region in a global perspective.

Last but not the least, I gratefully acknowledge the contribution of my beloved wife, Aloka, who helped in timely completion of the work by maintaining a conducive atmosphere at home. I likewise remain grateful to my affectionate mother who has always been a source of great inspiration to me.

ANSHUMAN GUPTA

Contents

1

Introduction

Seattle Round of WTO ended without producing any tangible result on account of dominance of disagreements over agreements among the member countries on the issues intended to be included in final agenda for the next round of negotiations. It put a brake on further progress of trade liberalisation under the multilateral agreements of WTO. Though the second attempt at Doha could break the stalemate only limited issues were agreed upon for negotiations. As a result, there would now be increased emphasis on strengthening regionalism through increasing trade within regional trading blocs. It would be in response to the realisation that increased co-operation among sovereign countries brings about more gains to the participating states, provided it is a positive-sum-game rather than a zero-sum-game.*

A term frequently used rather loosely to describe cooperation situation is the "Zero-sum-game." A game becomes zero-sum whenever two or more players compete for an outcome that only one of them can achieve. Such games are not trivial, and the consideration of them is not restricted to recreational past-times. For instance, in a territorial dispute, such as the case of Kashmir, the gain for one of the players implies an equivalent loss for the other. The sum of these outcomes is, therefore, zero.

Considering now a non-zero or positive-sum-game, co-operation by sovereign countries in economic sphere is generally of this category. When one points out that a given situation

---

* Zero–sum game and non-zero-sum game concepts are used in game theory. Many economists have used these concepts for economic co-operation among member countries of a regional trading blocs to show the benefits of non-zero-sum cooperation.

conforms to a non-zero sum game, he is, in fact, saying that cooperation in that situation can increase the size of the pie in a way that all participants can benefit in terms of improving their position in comparison to what it would be without such cooperation. It can, therefore, be seen that non-zero-sum game can offer possibilities of cooperation, whereas zero-sum game cannot.

The cooperation in economic field generally makes non-zero–sum game, as all the participating players stand to gain something, which is not possible without such cooperation. The economic cooperation through regional trading blocs (RTBs) increases trade among member countries as a result of withdrawal of or reduced trade barriers–tariff and non-tariff. It enlarges the size of market for the individual entrepreneurs of the member states. The entrepreneurs are able to experience economies of scale, which, in turn, scales down the cost per unit of production. The consumers get cheaper goods. Thus, the overall economic welfare of the member countries goes up. Moreover, it promotes specialisation in the region through encouraging the member states for adoption of the patterns of production based on their respective comparative advantages, thereby further contributing in reducing the price per unit of production and improving the quality. As a result of increase in competitiveness because of the combined effect of the economies of scale and specialisation, the entrepreneurs of a regional trading bloc would be able to export more outside the bloc. Furthermore, the entrepreneurs belonging to countries outside the bloc would have an incentive to invest in the member countries of the bloc to avoid the uneven playing field. It would further increase the production capacity as well as export capability of the member countries. Thus, it is a positive-sum-game or cooperation, in which all the players have a win-win situation.

The South Asian region, hitherto engrossed in the inconsequential territorial disputes, embarked on the non-zero-sum cooperation through forging the South Asian Association for Regional Cooperation (SAARC) in 1985. The purpose of SAARC was to promote all dimensional cooperation–social, political and economic–among member countries including India, Pakistan, Bangladesh, Sri Lanka, Bhutan, Nepal and Maldives. With the end of the cold war and the increased impetus to economic aspect of cooperation through regional arrangements the world over in 1990s, the SAARC also jumped onto the bandwagon by agreeing to establish a formal regional trading bloc with the conclusion of the SAARC Preferential Trading Arrangement (SAPTA) in 1993 Dhaka. After at reactification of the Agreement by the respective countries, the SAPTA came into being formally in 1995, the year in which economic cooperation through multilateral agreements also got strengthened with the advent of World Trade Organization (WTO).

Article XXIV of GATT, now WTO, permits regional trading blocs along with some qualifications. Many such groupings have emerged over the years. The significant ones, to name a few, include European Union (EU), North American Free Trade Agreement (NAFTA), Latin American Free Trade Association (LAFTA), Caribbean Common Market (CARICOM), Economic Community of Central African states (ECCAS), Gulf Cooperation Council (GCC), Association of South East Asian Nations (ASEAN), Asia Pacific Economic Cooperation, etc. In fact, RTBs always evoke controversies. Some economists are of the view that these RTBs are against the multilateral agreements under WTO, as they violate its Most Favoured Nation (MFN) clause. They discriminate between the members and non member countries while extending market access through giving concessions in tariff and non-tariff barriers to member states. It results in marginalisation of non-member countries, whereas the MFN clause, the soul of WTO, denies any kind of discrimination. They call it the blatant violation of WTO's MFN clause.

As far as another set of economists is concerned, they do not cast doubts over the compatibility of a RTB with WTO. They rather regard it as a facilitator to achieve the ultimate goal of WTO of frictionless trade among member countries. It is not advisable to withdraw trade barriers in the same time-frame for all the member countries of WTO on account of variation in their economic developmental levels. It is a good idea to first liberalise trade in a small group of countries with similar levels of economic advancement. This process would prepare them to face the bigger competition at the multilateral level. In fact, regional economic cooperation might serve as a precursor to multilateral cooperation under WTO especially for the developing countries. It enables member countries of a bloc to swim in the larger sea.

Many economists are of the view that the countries belonging to strong regional trading blocs with substantial intra-regional trade are at an advantageous position vis-à-vis the countries belonging to weak regional blocs with insignificant intra-bloc trade or having no affiliation to any bloc. This view is based on the premise that the member states of a strong regional trading bloc would be able to meet the major part of their import needs within the bloc through substantial trade creation by giving tariff and non-tariff concessions to its members, thereby driving out their close competitors hailing from outside the bloc. However, the countries having no membership in any bloc or affiliated to a weak one with unsubstantial intra-bloc trade might lose their markets in these strong regional blocs, while their imports will be of the same level or increasing over the period. This, in turn, would adversely affect the trade balance of these countries thereby worsening their Balance of Payment (BOP) position. While article XXIV of WTO imposes two conditions for setting up regional trading blocs, to what extent these conditions succeed in preventing marginalisation of the non-member countries is questionable. The first condition is that trade restrictions among countries forming the bloc must be eliminated over a period of normally not exceeding 10 years. They are not to be re-imposed later. The object of this condition is to ensure that a trading bloc is not used to merely circumvent the MFN clause. The second requirement is that the common external tariffs imposed after the formation of a bloc must not be greater than the average of the member countries existing before the formation of the bloc. It not only applies in the case of tariffs alone but also to non-tariff barriers. In practice, the efficacy of these conditions in minimizing the negative implications of establishing a bloc to the non-member countries seems doubtful.

Regional Trading Bloc: An Engine of Growth

A regional trading bloc, as has been amply demonstrated by several empirical studies, might serve as an engine for growth in the region as a whole. It provides an enlarged market to the entrepreneurs of the countries constituting a RTB. Its effects can be grouped into two categories–static effects accruing immediately or in the short-run and dynamic effects experienced in a relatively longer period. The static effects depend upon the trade creation and trade diversion. It is trade creation if a member country starts importing some product from another member country instead of producing it domestically after the formation of a bloc. The trade diversion, on the contrary, occurs when a member country starts importing a costlier good from another member country, which it earlier imported from outside the bloc before setting up the RTB. The adoption of common high tariff rates across all member states might render the goods coming from outside the bloc uncompetitive vis-a-vis ones originating from within the bloc. For instance, suppose India was importing something from outside the group at a rate of Rs. 20 per article–Rs. 10 as cost of the article and Rs. 10 as tariff- before the formation of the customs union. The same article costs Rs. 40–Rs. 30 as cost of the article and another Rs.10, as tariff–inside the group. After the formation of the customs union and imposing a common tariff of, say Rs. 30 per article, the cost of the article from outside the group would be Rs. 40, whereas inside the group, it would cost Rs. 30. It is a diversion of trade. The creation of trade is beneficial for the group as a whole as it increases welfare of the member states by providing them with cheaper goods, while the diversion of trade reduces the social welfare of the member states by forcing consumers to buy costlier goods.

In a static situation, if the trade creation is more than the trade diversion, it is always beneficial to form a bloc. Although economists can list a number of conditions for the static effects to go one way or the other on balance, it is not possible to say in general which of the two effects will be stronger. All that can be concluded, therefore, is indeterminacy.

Dynamic effects of forming a RTB are generally positive. Increased competition within the union leads to specialisation and the enlarged size of market permits economies of scale. These enhance the competitive edge of the entrepreneurs of the bloc. The most important dynamic effect is that investors from outside the group find it attractive to set up production facilities within the territory of the union to avoid the external trade barriers while operating in a single market. In the case of Europe, the dynamic effects of the customs union are considered to have been comparatively larger—six to seven times greater than the static effects. Thus, a RTB can serve as an engine for growth. Its significance increases manifold in the South Asian region, which is one of the least developed areas of the world.

Although South Asia accounts for about 20 percent of the world's population, its share in global GNP is mere 2 percent. Its contributions in the world imports and exports are about 1.3 percent and 0.8 percent respectively. It shows the extent of poverty and backwardness of the region. For most South Asian nations, domestic markets are small, and because of the absence of a good communication system, even they remain fragmented. As a result, it is not possible to make large investments and employ modern methods of production there. Some economists hold the view that much needed diversification of production cannot be achieved without an increase in the purchasing power of the people. For India and Pakistan, which have a sizable middle class, the situation might be somewhat different.

The current level of trade among the South Asian countries is very low. For instance, in 1997-98, the intra-bloc trade was a mere 4.3 percent of its total exports to the world. However, the percentage scaled up moderately to 4.9 percent in 1999-2000. It is far below the trade volume among the members of EU and NAFTA, which stood at 61.5 percent and 47.5 percent respectively in 1996. The figures for South Asia do not include the unofficial trade volumes, which are supposed to be higher between India and Bangladesh and India and Pakistan. As per one estimate, the unofficial trade between India and Pakistan was to the tune of $5 billion, which is five times the official trade figure. Some emotional dynamics rather than the business sense works against harnessing the full potential of trade and business cooperation between the two countries. It would be further testified by the fact that Pakistan has not yet accorded India the Most Favoured Nation (MFN) Status even after over five years of WTO coming into existence. India had granted the MFN status to Pakistan in 1995 itself. Pakistan still had the restricted list of importable items from India comprising just 573 items till 1995. However, under the second round of SAPTA negotiations, Pakistan announced concessional tariffs for India on several items, which were over and above the restricted list, bringing the total number of items in the list of importables to 601. In its 1997-98-trade policy, Pakistan identified another 14 items for import from India, increasing the list to 615 items.

To improve the economic ties between the two countries, an institutional arrangement at the level of industry associations of the two countries was forged just after the historic Lahore Bus journey of Prime Minister Atal Bihari Vajpayee in 1999. Federation of Indian Chamber of Commerce and Industry (FICCI) and Federation of Pakistan Chamber of Commerce and Industry (FPCCI) joined hands to set up India-Pakistan Chamber of Commerce and Industry (IPCCI) in April 1999. Though the bilateral trade between the two countries has been showing an increasing trend in the 1990s, it has been much below the potential. In 1990, India's exports to Pakistan were just Rs. 73.60 crore while imports were Rs. 84.49 crore. In 1995, exports grew to Rs. 256.19 crore and imports to Rs. 150.80 crore. Further, in 1999-2000 Indian exports to Pakistan increased to Rs. 405.35 crore and imports, to Rs. 296.74 crore.

Several factors are responsible for this state of affairs. First, the historical unpleasant instances including the partition of India on the basis of religion to form the new state of Pakistan and then break-up of Pakistan to carve out Bangladesh in 1971, and India's role in this movement, coupled with persistent territorial conflicts especially among the three countries have resulted in the adoption of restrictive, even discriminatory trade practices against each other. These practices, as often as not, defy the economic sense. Second, there has not been the free flow of information across the South Asian countries, which leads to lack of knowledge about each other's products and the import and export baskets. Third, over the years, the countries of the region have followed the policy of import substitution in a bid to become self- reliant. As a result, their economies have turned out to be more competitive than complementary. One estimate suggests that although two-thirds of the exports of most South Asian nations today comprise manufactured goods, the major portions of them originate in food and textile sectors. Fourth, a SAARC study on the subject has estimated that 40 to 70 percent of imports of the region are financed through foreign assistance and invisible earnings. They do not consider it worthwhile to divert a major part of it for procurement within the region. Fifth and finally, more than 50 percent of imports of the South Asian countries comprise capital goods, machinery, food and petroleum products. These are the items that are neither produced in large quantities within South Asia, nor are their quality and price attractive.

It is generally argued that RTBs are not successful in developing countries on account of lack of complementarities among them. They are more or less at the same stage of economic development, mainly dominated by the agricultural sector and the industries involving low level technology. Since they lie within the same latitudinal position limiting their climatic variation except in the case of mountainous or coastal terrain, they end up with producing similar agricultural items. In industrial sector too, they mainly have agro-based and unsophisticated technology involving industries, which restrict their attempt of infusing product differentiation in products. All these factors militate against making a RTB successful. Among the developed countries, on the contrary, a RTB becomes more successful for its having in-built advantages. As these developed countries have advanced technology- based industries, like automobiles, capital goods, knowledge-based industries, etc. they are able to produce a range of varieties of the same product. They generally specialise in one or two varieties of a product and exchange others between each other. It helps create trade among them, whereas in the case of developing countries, there are more chances of trade diversion. However, this conclusion has been challenged. Critics of this argue that the criterion of ascertaining whether the altered position as a result of the formation of a bloc among developing countries is trade diversion or trade creation for a country should be different. If it results in the establishment of infant industries in a member country for some items, it would be trade creation for it. If, on the contrary, it facilitates their setting up in some other member country, it would be diversion of trade for the former country. Thus, the establishment of infant industries in one's own country is trade creation, while in other member countries, it would be trade diversion.

The regional economic integration scheme is not effected in one stroke. Instead it is a matter of evolution. In the continuum scale of evolution of a RTB, Preferential Trading Arrangement lies at the starting point, while an Economic and Currency Union comes at the last stage. In between these two extreme points, there are other stages of evolution including Free Trade Area, Customs Union and Common Market in sequence. The SAPTA is at the first stage, while the EU has almost completed the evolution process with its common currency and well-coordinated monetary and fiscal policies of the member countries.

The work has been divided into six chapters including introduction as the first chapter. The second chapter deals with the evolution of SAARC as an institution, besides studying the structural transformation of the SAARC economies during 1980s and 90s and their cooperation especially in the economic sphere.

The third chapter studies the conditions for establishing RTBs under the WTO regime, economic rationale of forming regional blocs and the comparison between the RTBs among the developed countries and developing countries. It also attempts to explore possibility of any perceived contradiction between multilateral cooperation under WTO and regional cooperation under a RTB.

The fourth chapter examines the provisions of the Agreement, which set up the SAPTA in 1995. In the fifth chapter, the progress made by the SAPTA so far has been evaluated. The final sixth chapter contains an overall appraisal of the SAPTA along with some recommendations for its improved performance and upgrading into a Free Trade Area for the South Asian region.

2

Regional Cooperation under SAARC (1985-95)

South Asian countries share strong cultural ties and linkages going back to antiquity. South Asian languages, music, art, painting, theatre, and food have woven abiding regional ties having both creative and spiritual dimensions. Even after the partition of India on the basis of religion in 1947, Islam has, numerically speaking, a larger presence in India in comparison with Pakistan. Even after 50 years of separate existence, the two major countries of the region (India and Pakistan) share many common cultural traditions. Culture has diverse and even magical ways of uniting people. The people of South Asia realise this fact, and this realisation becomes even more conspicuous when they meet outside the region.

The countries of the region not only have common cultural ties, rooted in history, but also many common socio-economic problems affecting the whole region. A majority of the countries of the region have adopted the democratic system of governance and are at different stages of evolution of the democratic process. Pakistan and Bhutan are, however, exception in this regard. In Pakistan, the democratic process has had several setbacks with the military rulers usurping power repeatedly. In Bhutan, it is still a monarchy. Given below are some of the most acute problems faced by the countries of the region.

High Population Growth

The single most important problem affecting almost all South Asian countries, except Sri Lanka, is high population growth. Almost one- fourth of the world population resides in this region making it one of the highest densely-populated regions of the world. The high population growth is responsible for the slow increase in per capita income, heavy burden on natural resources and environmental degradation at all levels including land, water and air. It is also responsible for perpetuating many economic and social ills.

Slow Economic Growth

The South Asian region is regarded as one of the most underdeveloped regions of the world having almost half of its population (almost 600 million) below the poverty line. The average per capita income in the countries of the region is below $500, with Sri Lanka having the highest—$740 in 1996[1]. Behind this low per capita income lie enormous disparities.

It is necessary to have a reasonably high rate of economic growth to combat poverty and deprivation in the region. The states of the region, on the contrary, have continuously experienced a low rate of growth on account of many reasons. Besides their production baskets having mainly agriculture goods, they include low level of services and less-valued manufactured items. Although India and Sri Lanka have relatively advanced and diversified industrial structures, their persistent inward-looking policies (until recently) impeding the export growth and negating the economies of scale, continuance of License Raj resulting in a distorted and flawed growth of industries and the excessive role of government in managing the economic activities leading to low level of productivity, results in slow overall economic growth. The average growth rate had been at about 5.5 per cent in 1980s, which moved up to the higher bracket of 6 to 7 per cent in 1990s, as most of the economies of the region implemented far-reaching economic reform measures during this period[2]. However, it is still far below the growth rates recorded by China and South East Asian countries and certainly not enough to fight the extent of poverty prevailing in the region.

High Illiteracy

The region has the highest number of illiterates of the world. In spite of the efforts put in to improve the position by the states of the region, over 40 per cent of the total population is still illiterate, with female average being over 50 per cent. Sri Lanka is an exception in this regard. Literacy, especially among the females, is highly correlated with low fertility, higher income and increased productivity. However, India has improved its literacy rate (above 60 per cent) of late with the concerted efforts of the government, private sector and non-governmental organisations (NGOs).

Infant Mortality

Infant mortality rate is directly related to health problems in a country, its literacy rate, level of per capita income, etc. Since the South Asian countries have fared badly on all these counts, the infant mortality rate in these countries, except Sri Lanka, is very high. Infant mortality rate in India in 1997 was 71 per thousand live births. It was 90 in Pakistan, 78 in Nepal and 77 in Bangladesh[3].

Flaws in Governance

Although all countries of the region, except Pakistan and Bhutan, have embraced the democratic system of governance, they are afflicted with many common maladies though in varying degrees. Nepal, which was an absolute monarchy, also adopted democracy close on the heels of East European countries switching over to democratic system during the late 80s and early 90s. Though the monarchy is still there, the monarch works as a constitutional head of the state. The executive powers are vested in the Cabinet responsible to an elected legislature. In case of Pakistan, although its citizens started with a taste of democracy, the process has been disturbed intermittently by the powerful Military Junta in the country. It happened in 1999 also when the Army Chief, General Parvez Musharaff, deposed the elected government of Nawaz Sharief. India and Sri Lanka are relatively mature and stable democracies. Bangladesh, though presently it has a popular government, remains vulnerable to turmoil as it was itself carved out of Pakistan after a prolonged struggle. Bhutan still follows a monarchical system.

Even the best democracy of the region-the Indian- is plagued with many serious problems warranting urgent corrective measures. All the democratic institutions—legislature, cabinet and judiciary—have degenarated over the years. They do not seem to discharge properly the duties assigned to them by the Constitution, but are more concerned with the personal or parochial interests at the cost of the electorate.

Among other common problems afflicting the region as a whole are the rise of ethnic conflicts, escalation of violence, unplanned growth of urbanisation, degradation of environment and corruption in public life.

Having looked into the common features, both positive and negative, shared by the states of South Asian region, it is but appropriate to analyse the kind of relationship existing between these countries, which is by no means a rosy one. More often than not, the states of the region have been immersed in the inconsequential territorial zero-sum disputes. They have not yet recognised the importance of non-zero sum cooperation. India and Pakistan have already fought three full-fledged wars, not to mention the fourth—a limited one in Kargil in 1999. Kashmir remains the bone of contention between the two countries. Pakistan has now been engaged in cross- border terrorism in Kashmir for more than a decade. It has only further deepened the already existing distrust between the two neighbouring countries locked in a dispute over Kashmir since 1947. Their defence outlays have swelled to astronomical levels. In the year 1990-91, the defence outlay for the region as per cent age of GDP stood at 3.5 per cent, which was up from 2.8 per cent in 1960. Pakistan's military expenditure was the highest in the region as the proportion of GDP at 6.5 per cent, followed by Sri Lanka (4.8 per cent), India (3.1 per cent), Nepal (1.6 per cent) and Bangladesh (1.4 per cent) in 1990-91[4].

When all major countries of the world are taking steps towards denuclearisation and curtailing their defence outlays, India and Pakistan have escalated the arms race by testing the nuclear bombs in 1998. With the failure of the Agra Summit (July 2001) between the two countries, their defence expenditure is likely to grow in the times to come. Likewise, Pakistan and Bangladesh, and Bangladesh and India have problems. Their defence expenditures can be minimised and channeled into some developmental activities through fostering all round regional cooperation in South Asia.

A beginning in this direction was made by leaders of the region with the conclusion of an agreement in 1985 to set up the South Asian Association for Regional Cooperation (SAARC). It is a regional organisation with its secretariat in Kathmandu, Nepal. The SAARC was set up to accelerate the process of economic, social and cultural development and promote and strengthen collective self-reliance through joint action in certain agreed areas of cooperation. The following objectives were included in the Charter of the SAARC Agreement:

- promotion of the welfare of citizens of South Asia by improving their quality of life,
- acceleration of economic growth, social progress and cultural development in the region and providing all individuals the opportunity to live in dignity to realize their full potential,
- promoting and strengthening collective self-reliance among the countries of South Asia,
- contribution to mutual trust, understanding and appreciation of each others' problems,
- promotion of active collaboration and mutual assistance in the economic, social, cultural, technical and scientific fields,
- strengthening cooperation with other developing countries,

- forging cooperation among themselves in the international forums on matters of common interests and
- cooperation with international and regional organisations with similar aims and purposes.

The leaders of the region decided not to include disputed bilateral issues between the countries of the region in the SAARC forum. The SAARC Charter has also indicated the principles that should govern regional cooperation in various fields. These are:

- cooperation within the framework of the SAARC shall be based on respect for the principles of sovereign equality, territorial integrity, political independence, non-interference in the internal affairs of other States and mutual benefits,
- such cooperation shall not be a substitute for bilateral and multilateral cooperation but shall complement them, and
- such cooperation shall not be inconsistent with bilateral and multilateral obligations.

It is thus clear that the SAARC forum was established to have multi-faceted cooperation among the member countries. This kind of regional cooperation is not a substitute to the existing bilateral as well as multilateral agreements. Rather, it is supplementary to them. The Charter provided for a Standing Committee and a number of Technical Committees, whose terms of reference covered areas like determination of the potential and the scope of regional cooperation in various fields and the formulation of programmes and preparation of projects in different sectors. The Charter envisaged that the spirit of regional cooperation should get itself translated into concrete programmes and the projects on the basis of detailed deliberation among experts of all the member countries specialising in different technical fields. In order to facilitate the organisation and coordination of these activities, an independent SAARC Secretariat was set up in Kathmandu. It started functioning from

January 1987. The process of regional cooperation among SAARC countries is achieved through the "Integrated Programme of Action"(IPA). There are twelve agreed areas of cooperation under IPA, which include Agriculture, Communications, Education and Culture, Environment, Health and Population, Meteorology, Prevention of Drug Trafficking and Drug Abuse, Rural Development, Service and Technology, Tourism, Transport and Women in Development. Each of these areas is being looked after by a Technical Committee having experts in the respective fields in the member countries. The Technical Committees meet once a year to decide about the programmes. Seminars, workshops and the training programmes are held in the member countries for exchange of information. An overall review of the work done by the various committees is given below.[5]

Technical Committee on Agriculture

Several measures have been initiated under this Committee since its first meeting in 1983. Since agriculture is the main occupation across the SAARC member countries, even though contribution of agriculture sector to GNP in the region has declined to 24.7 per cent in 1997 from 37.8 per cent in 1980, decisions in this Committee have far-reaching implications for the overall development of the region. This Technical Committee played a vital role in establishing the SAARC Agricultural Information Centre (SAIC) in Bangladesh in 1988. The ground-level partnerships have resulted in the inter-country exchange of germplasm and breeding materials of livestock and fishery in accordance with countries' respective quarantine regulations. Exchange of prototypes of farm tools and equipment for trials and adaptation has given tremendous advantage to the agriculture community in the member states. Breeding programmes for stepping up productivity of rice and wheat have been undertaken and multi-location trials for various crops are underway. Besides, various activities have been organised relating to integrated forestry management, promotion of bio-villages, training of farmers and farm women, promotion of income-generating projects such as bee–keeping, sericulture, mushroom production, networking arrangement on soil and water management, etc. Of-late, the Committee has emphasised evolving an 'Agricultural Perspective for South Asia up to the Year 2020'. It focuses on developing comprehensive investment strategies, appropriate technologies and human resources.

Technical Committee on Communication

The Technical Committees on Telecommunications and Postal Services, set up in 1983, were merged into one in 1993. The Committee has taken many significant measures including training of professionals, improving rural telecommunications, providing ISD, automatic telex and bureaufax services, improving inter-country links, evolving professional postal management course and electronic tracking, setting up of a South Asian Information Network, postal marketing, etc. More recently, a Memorandum of Understanding has been signed between the International Telecommunication Union and SAARC to improve the quality of telecommunications and telematic services in the region. A notable achievement in a related area has been the adoption by the SAARC Information Ministers of an eighteen-point Plan of Action to facilitate free flow of information in the region. Besides creation of a web page for exchange of news agencies of SAARC member countries (SMCs), this includes exploring the feasibility of setting up a SAARC Information Centre with Media Production, Research and Training Units, and creation of a SAARC Media Development Fund.

Technical Committee on Environment and Meteorology

The Technical Committees on meteorology and environment were combined into one in 1996. The Committee has evolved several modalities to implement pollution control and hazardous waste management programme. Exchange of low cost and environmentally sound technologies and strengthening of environment management infrastructure are being given considerable attention. The various aspects of environment, like green-house effect, climate change, role of women in sustainable development, environmental legislation and its management, wildlife management, cooperation in floral and faunal bio-diversity, agrometeorology, climatology, data exchange, instrumentation and predictability of monsoonal rain and flooding. In this regard, SAARC Meteorological Research Centre (SMRC) has been playing a vital role.

As a significant development, the SAARC Environmental Ministers Conference was held in 1992 to take a combined stand at the UN Conference on Environment and Development (UNCED). Similarly, their meeting (1997) to coordinate their position before the Special Session of UN General Assembly to review Agenda 21 is a major achievement of the SAARC cooperation process. Subsequently, the Ministers also met to prepare an Action Plan, which *interalia* included preparation of a SAARC State of the Environment Report by the end of 1999.

Technical Committee on Science and Technology

Set up in 1983, the Committee covers a wide range of areas for cooperation including various training programmes for scientists and technologists on tannery waste management, low cost housing, development of prawn hatcheries, electronics and molecular biology. A major achievement of this Committee has been in terms of carrying out joint research projects in areas such as design and manufacture of food processing equipment and appropriate post-harvest food technology for perishable items. Besides, a number of state- of- art reports have been prepared on bio-gas, mineral resources exploration, remote sensing techniques, etc. Modalities of effecting cooperation are being made in several other areas such as solar and thermal technology, standardization of thermal devices, energy modelling with special reference to rural areas, astronomy and astrophysics, bio-processing of food and enzymes, building materials and technologies, rural technologies, food processing technologies and biotechnology.

Technical Committee on Rural Development

Rural development has been accorded a special emphasis in the SAARC framework. Its Technical Committee has organised several training programmes and interactive sessions covering areas like rural energy, disaster management, rural water supply, employment generation, etc. Other activities under his Committee included studying the role of NGOs in rural development, enhancing production credit for rural women, rural employment in non-farm sector, rural housing and transfer of technology, establishment of SHELTER Information Network (SHELTERNET), creation of assets and enhancement of availability of credit and human resource development.

Technical Committee on Tourism

Ever since its establishment in 1991, the Technical Committee on tourism is making efforts to develop the SAARC region as an attractive destination for tourism. To achieve this end, a web site on Tourism in South Asia is being developed under its aegis. Other initiatives include, developing joint tour packages, SAARC travel guide, joint participation in international tourism fairs and a SAARC Scheme for Promotion of Organized Tourism. Possibilities of evolving framework agreements of cooperation with World Tourism Organization and Pacific Asia Travel Association are also being worked out.

A significant development in this direction was the launching of eight training packages produced by the South Asia Integrated Tourism Human Resource Development Programme (SAITHRDP) at the SAARC Tourism Ministerial Meeting held in Colombo in September 1997. The SAITHRDP is a joint initiative of the public and private sectors in the SAARC countries. It is supported by the European Commission.

Technical Committee on Women in Development

Established in 1986, the Technical Committee on Women in Development Process organises many activities including preparation of a Regional Plan of Action for Women, dissemination of technical information on gender issues and publication of journals on specific themes relating to women in development. It is worth mentioning that a combined stand was taken by the SAARC countries at the fourth World Conference on Women in Beijing in 1995.

Technical Committee on Transport

Various measures have been taken under this Technical Committee since its establishment in 1983. Efforts are on to improve the transport infrastructure in the region by upgrading land, sea and air transport linkages. Several training courses have been offered in the fields of corporate planning for railway sector and highway and bridge engineering. Several other initiatives under consideration relate to joint ventures operation for container liner shipping services for long haul trade routes, joint ventures in consultancy, contracting and other related services and flight safety oversight programme.

Other Cooperation under SAARC

Measures have also been initiated to strengthen the scientific technical base in the region. Four SAARC Regional Institutes have been established. These include SAARC Agriculture Information Centre and SAARC Meteorological Research Centre in Dhaka, SAARC Tuberculosis Centre in Kathmandu and the SAARC Documentation Centre in New Delhi. Attempts are also being made to develop a coordinating arrangement with research institutes in various fields in the member countries instead of establishing a regional institute in each field due to financial constraints.

The Sixth SAARC Summit (1991) brought poverty eradication to the centre-stage of regional cooperation. It set up an

Independent South Asian Commission on Poverty Alleviation (ISACPA). The subsequent Summit (1993) focused on poverty eradication from the region by the year 2002 through an agenda of action based upon the strategy of social mobilisation, policy of decentralised agricultural development and small scale labour-intensive industrialisation and human development. The Eighth SAARC Summit (1995) adopted recommendations of the Finance/Planning Ministers to establish a three-tier mechanism for exchanging information on poverty eradication. The first tier includes the secretaries to the respective SAARC governments in different ministries concerned with poverty eradication and social development. The second-tier is formed by the Finance and Planning Secretaries of the member countries. At the third tier, Finance and Planning Ministers of the countries meet to review the developments at the first two tiers. In the various meetings of the different tiers, the need to view the poverty eradication in the overall context of development strategy was emphasised.

The SAARC has underscored the need for building people-to- people contact in the region. This has been sought with the help of several initiatives, such as the SAARC Audio Visual Exchange (SAVE) Programme, SAARC Scheme for Promotion of Organised Tourism, SAARC Youth Volunteers Programmes (SYVOP), etc. These Programmes have helped in maintaining the cultural and social linkages among the people of the region.

Besides the governmental initiatives, many steps have been taken at the non-governmental level to strengthen the institutional framework in the South Asian region. Mention may be made of the institutions like Independent Group of South Asian Cooperation (IGSAC), SAARC Economic Association, Coalition for Action on South Asian Cooperation (CASAC) and Indian Council for South Asian Cooperation.

Trade and Economic Cooperation among SAARC Nations

Various SAARC-level funds have been established. Significant among them are the SAARC-Japan Special Fund and the South

Asian Development Fund (SADF). The SADF is a three-window fund with the merger of SAARC Fund for Regional Projects and the SAARC Regional Fund and a third window for social development and infrastructure development.

Economic cooperation being the key to any successful regional grouping got impetus with the preparation of national level studies by the member countries. It made the synthesis report of SAARC secretariat (1991), now commonly known as TMS (Trade and Manufactures Services) study on cooperation. From the Indian side, the study was made by the Research and Information System (RIS) for the Non-Aligned and other Developing Countries in 1990. The RIS Study made a number of policy recommendations to promote the SAARC economic cooperation. They were, *inter alia*, setting up of a Project Development Facility, SAARC Council of Development Finance Institutions, launching of a SAARC Preferential Trading Arrangement (SAARC-PTA) and formation of SAARC Chambers of Commerce and Industry.

Before analysing the economic cooperation, especially trade, among the SAARC countries before the formation of SAPTA in 1995, it would be worthwhile to critically study the varied structures of the SAARC economies. The structures of member countries' economies of a regional trading bloc influence a great deal the level of economic cooperation among them. The industrially advanced economies have more scope for economic cooperation than agriculture–based less developed economies. There is high complementarity among the industrially advanced economies owing to their employing sophisticated technology giving scope for product differentiation. There are less chances for product differentiation in the agriculture-based economies or the economies dominated by the traditional industries using the low-level technology. The difference in cooperation between the industrially advanced economies and developing economies having largely the agriculture sector and weak industrial structure have been discussed at length in the later chapters.

The South Asian economies are undergoing a process of gradual structural transformation. This process got an impetus in 1990s owing to many far-reaching measures initiated by these economies. A gradual, but definite, shift in the paradigm of managing economies from mainly government-controlled economic activities to one where private sector has a major role to play is underway. The forces of a market economy —demand and supply—are being unshackled to play a free role. Besides almost dismantling the License Raj and the replacement of orthodox import substitution policies with outward-looking export-promoting ones, the important measures implemented by most of the South Asian economies especially during 1990s include, moving to market-determined exchange rate policy and scaling down the direct and indirect taxes. Other significant steps are reforming the financial sector to make it more vibrant and competitive to cater to the needs of post-liberalised economies and inviting foreign investments (portfolio and direct investments both) to fill up the gap between the required capital and current saving rates. All these steps cumulatively resulted in the improved productivity especially in the industrial sector and, resultantly, higher overall economic growth in 1990s. The average annual economic growth rate for the whole SAARC region during period 1994-97 was 6.4 per cent as compared to 5.8 per cent recorded during 1980s. During 1994-97, India had the highest average annual economic growth rate of 7 per cent, followed by Maldives (6.6 per cent).

Most of the SAARC countries have traditionally been dominated by the agriculture sector, although the share of agriculture in GDP has dwindled of late to 24.8 per cent in 1997 from 37.8 per cent in 1980 for the SAARC region. However, the agriculture sector still employs over 60 per cent of the region's population. The contributions of industrial and services sectors to GDP have increased to 30.2 per cent and 45 per cent in 1997 from 25 per cent and 37.2 per cent respectively in 1980.[6] This change in the composition of GDPs in SAARC countries is shown in Table 2.1.

TABLE 2.1
Sectoral Composition of GDP in SAARC Countries

(As per cent of GDP)

Region/ Country	Agriculture		Industry		Services	
	1980	1997	1980	1997	1980	1997
SAARC	37.8	24.8	25.0	30.2	37.2	45.0
Bangladesh	49.4	32.4	14.8	19.2	35.8	48.4
Bhutan	56.7	36.2	12.2	28.0	31.1	35.9
India	38.1	24.3	25.9	31.9	36.0	43,8
Maldives	31.0	22.0	6.0	17.0	63.0	61.0
Nepal	61.8	41.0	11.9	19.1	26.3	39.8
Pakistan	30.6	24.2	25.6	26.4	43.8	49.4
Sri Lanka	26.6	18.3	27.2	32.3	46.2	49.4

Source: ADB, Asia Development Outlook, 1997 and 1998.

As is obvious from the Table 2.1, the share of agriculture in GDP is decreasing over the period 1980-97 across all member countries of SAARC. It is, in fact, the result of various developmental activities taken up by the respective governments of the region in the industrial and services sectors, coupled with many path-breaking measures effected in the economies of the region to promote the private entrepreneurs in these sectors. Although the dependence on agriculture sector is relatively lower in case of large and medium-sized economies than other economies of the region, the share of the sector has declined at a faster rate in small economies than others. However, it still contributes almost a quarter of GDP in South Asia.

The industrial sector, regarded as an engine of growth, has seen a moderate rise in its contribution to GDP over the past one and a half decades. The share of this sector in GDP of the region rose from 25 per cent in 1980s to 30.2 per cent in 1997. The two land-locked countries, viz. Nepal and Bhutan, and island economies, especially Maldives, have recorded a more impressive rise in the share of industry than other countries of the region.

The share of the services sector in GDP of the SAARC nations as a whole was almost the same as that of agriculture in 1980. However, the contribution of agriculture has declined over the period 1980-97 and the size of services sector share in GDP has grown rapidly during this period, even more briskly than that of industrial sector in the region. From 37.2 per cent of the total production of the region in 1980s, services sector expanded fast to register 45 per cent share of GDP in 1997.[7] Traditionally, the island countries in the region are more dependent on this sector because of vast potential of these economies in tourism-related activities.

Analysing the individual sectors' contribution to GDP in each country of the region in 1997, the contribution of agriculture sector was the highest in Nepal (41 per cent), whereas it was lowest in Sri Lanka at 18.3 per cent. In case of India and Pakistan, the share of the sector in GDP was 24.3 per cent and 24.2 per cent respectively. The biggest decline in the share of agriculture in GDP over the period 1980-97 has been recorded by Bhutan (36 per cent), followed by Bangladesh (34 per cent).

The share of industry in GDP was the highest in Sri Lanka (32 per cent) and the lowest (17 per cent) in Maldives in 1997. The industry's contribution to GDP in Bhutan, Bangladesh, India, Nepal, and Pakistan was 28 per cent, 19.2 per cent, 31.9 per cent, 19.1 per cent and 26.4 per cent respectively in 1997.

As far as the services sector is concerned, it can be clearly noticed from the Table that the share of this sector in GDP is growing at a rapid pace for the region. It had the largest share in GDP among all three sectors in countries of the region, except in Bhutan and Nepal, in 1997. The services sector accounted for nearly 50 per cent of GDP in Bangladesh, Pakistan, and Sri Lanka in 1997. Maldives has secured the highest contribution from this sector to its GDP among all countries of the region–as high as 61 per cent. For Bhutan, India and Nepal, it stood at 35.9 per cent, 43.8 per cent and 39.8 per cent respectively in the same year.

Analysing further the individual sectors of countries of the region, measures taken to increase their productivity and their respective performance, especially in the last decade, the following trends can be observed.

Agriculture Sector

The agriculture sector has seen the erratic growth performance during the period 1990-97 across all countries of the region. There are many common problems with varying intensity plaguing the agriculture sector in countries of the region. In addition to the small-sized holdings of arable land, the more important ones among these include over- reliance on monsoon and inadequate irrigation facilities, insufficiency of the institutional credit, absence of proper marketing facilities, poor and inadequate storage facilities, high level of illiteracy among farmers and lack of derivative markets in farm commodities to hedge the risk element of farmers. All these factors are combinedly hindering the growth of the sector. However, over 60 per cent of total population of the region is still engaged in this profession. This excessive employment in agriculture is the cause of under-employment in the sector pulling down the overall productivity per worker in the region. Although several measures have already been taken to correct this position, many other significant ones are still to be taken. In the Table 2.2, the growth performance of the countries of the region in agriculture has been shown.

The average annual growth rate of the agriculture sector for the whole region was 2.5 per cent during the period 1981-90, which declined marginally to 2.3 per cent during 1991-97. The average rate further declined to 2.2 per cent during 1994-97 with Coefficient of Variation (C.V.) being 1.8 showing high fluctuations. The lowest growth (0.9 per cent) was recorded in 1997.

TABLE-2.2

Growth Performance of Agriculture Sector in SAARC Countries

(Per cent per annum)

Region/Country	Ave. 1980-90	Ave. 1991-97	1994	1995	1996	1997	Ave. 1994-97	S.D. 1994-97	C.V. 1994-97
SAARC	2.5	2.3	4.4	–1.4	6.7	–0.9	2.2	3.9	1.8
Bangladesh	0.9	2.9	0.3	–1.0	3.7	6.0	2.5	3.1	1.2
Bhutan	2.1	3.3	3.9	4.0	6.4	4.1	4.6	1.2	0.26
India	2.5	2.1	4.6	–3.0	7.9	–2.0	1.9	5.2	2.7
Maldives	1.4	1.9	2.6	1.5	—	—	—	—	—
Nepal	1.4	2.3	7.6	–0.3	4.4	4.1	3.9	3.2	0.82
Pakistan	3.4	3.9	5.2	6.6	5.3	0.7	4.5	2.6	0.58
Sri Lanka	2.2	1.8	3.3	3.3	–4.6	5.4	1.9	4.4	2.3

Source: ADB—Asian Development Outlook, various issues.

Notes: S.D.—Standard Deviation.

C.V.—Coefficient of Variation- Standard Deviation/ Mean

Analysing the position individually for each country, Bangladesh had an average annual growth rate of 2.9 per cent during 1991-97, compared to 0.9 per cent during 1980s. During 1994-97, it recorded slightly lower mean annual growth rate of 2.5 per cent with C.V. being 1.2 reflecting the high variability in growth rates. The agriculture sector in Bangladesh suffers from excessive dependence on monsoon, the use of obsolete farm management techniques and lack of quality agricultural inputs. Bhutan, largely dependent on subsistence agriculture, forestry and livestock, registered average annual growth rate of 3.3 per cent during 1991-97, which was up from 2.1 per cent achieved during 1980s. The average further improved when calculated for the period 1994-97. It was 4.6 per cent with very low fluctuation as C.V. was 0.26. The average growth rate of Bhutan's agriculture sector (3.3 per cent) was higher than that of South Asian region (2.3 per cent) as a whole during the period 1991-97.

The growth rate of agriculture in India averaged at 2.1 per cent a year during 1991-97 compared to 2.5 per cent during 1980s. It again slightly fell to 1.9 per cent during 1994-97. It had high variation as C.V. was calculated at 2.7. In spite of many corrective measures effected over the years and having experienced one green revolution, the agriculture sector in India is still afflicted with many serious problems. In addition to the small level of holdings of agriculture land, they are inadequate institutional credit, restriction on inter- state movements of agriculture items, poor and insufficient storage and warehouse facilities, low coverage of arable land under irrigation, pathetic market facilities, etc., to name a few.

In Maldives, fisheries and tourism are the main occupations influencing the overall growth rate of the economy to a large extent. In the two periods, 1981-1990 and 1991-97, the average growth rate of the agriculture sector improved moderately from 1.4 per cent to 1.9 per cent respectively. However, it is much lower than that of the region's agriculture sector as a whole. Nepal, having the largest agriculture sector in relation to GDP in the region, secured 2.3 per cent average annual growth rate during

1991-97 compared to 1.4 per cent during 1980s. Its annual mean further scaled up to 3.9 per cent during 1994-97. The C.V. for the same period was 0.82 reflecting a relatively low fluctuation.

In Pakistan, many policy reforms were undertaken in respect to agriculture sector during the last two decades. It recorded an impressive average annual growth rate of 3.9 per cent during 1991-97, which is an improvement over the annual mean of 3.4 per cent registered during 1980s. Its average further increased to 4.5 per cent with low fluctuation (C.V. .58) during 1994-97. The agriculture contribution to GDP is the lowest in Sri Lanka among all the members of SAARC. The Sri Lankan economy is dominated by three plantation crops–tea, rubber and coconut. It has seen a highly volatile growth performance of the sector during 1990s. Its average annual growth rate was 1.8 per cent in 1991-97 as compared to 2.2 per cent during 1980s. During 1994-97, its average moved up marginally to 1.9 per cent with high level of variability as C.V. being 2.3.

Industrial Sector

The performance of the industrial sector has been varied across the SAARC member countries during 1991-97. Bhutan recorded the highest annual average growth rate of 9.4 per cent, whereas Pakistan had the lowest (5.2 per cent) during the period. In fact, the 1990s have been an eventful period for the South Asian economies in particular and world economy in general. It is a worth-remembering decade for most of the South Asian countries. On tracing back the economic history of these countries, one would find that the major reform measures on the economic front, especially in the industrial sector, have been initiated during this period. The significant ones comprised unshackling the industries from the License Raj, implementing the export-promotional policies rather than the import substitution ones followed earlier, moving into the low tax rates regime by reducing the corporation tax and excise and import duties, initiating gradually the market-determined exchange rate and liberalising the foreign investment regulations. The process of disintermediation in the financial sector has been expedited to make it more vibrant and cost-effective. However, besides poor infrastructure (road, power, port, telecommunication, etc.), still many common maladies infecting the industrial sector in general in all the countries of the region include, higher import duties on raw materials in comparison to those prevailing in U.S.A., Western Europe and even South East Asian countries, high rates of interest, inefficient financial market, etc. All these factors cumulatively result in the high cost economies, which, in turn, render the products originating from these economies uncompetitive vis-a-vis items coming from elsewhere. These are also responsible for the region's inability to attract substantial amount of foreign direct investment (FDI) in spite of its having liberal FDI-governing rules for almost a decade. It was merely about 5 per cent of the total FDI coming into Asia as a whole in 1997.[8]

Another memorable event of the last decade was the busting of the erstwhile Asian tigers—South East Asian economies. The miracle economies, as they were considered to be earlier, were reduced to almost half in terms of their GDPs in dollars in the wake of the financial crisis in 1997-98. It was, in fact, the currency crisis, which first started in July 1997 in Thailand and then quickly engulfed the other countries of the region, especially South Korea, Malaysia and Indonesia. The currencies of these countries got depreciated by over 50 per cent in the case of Malaysia and Philippines, over 75 per cent in Korea and Thailand and by 299 per cent in the case of Indonesia in the course of just few months.[9] The currencies of the SAARC countries were rather stable over this period with the extent of depreciation being under 11 per cent over the comparable period. It was because of the fact that economies of the SAARC region were not yet fully integrated with the world economy. They still do not have full convertibility of their currencies. Hence, the SAARC nations have not been directly affected by the currency crisis in the East and South East Asia.

Table 2.3 shows the industrial performance of the individual countries of the region for the period 1980-1997.

The average annual growth rate of the industrial sector in the SAARC region was 5.7 per cent during 1980s, which increased to 6.5 per cent during the period 1991-97. During 1994-97, the average growth improved further to 8.2 per cent with low fluctuation in growth rates during the period (C.V. 0.36). The industrial average annual growth rate in Bangladesh declined during 1991-97 in comparison to 1980s from 7.1 per cent to 6.4 per cent. For the period 1994-97, the average further declined marginally to 6.3 per cent, with low variability as C.V. being 0.35. Jute continues to be the major industry of the country. The other upcoming manufacturing industries include readymade garments, chemicals, leather, food processing and basic metals.

Bhutan, having the fastest growing industrial sector in the region, secured 9.9 per cent and 9.4 per cent average annual growth rates during 1980s and 1991-97 respectively. During 1994-97, the mean growth rate was 10.2 per cent with C. V. 0.66, which indicates a high level of variation in growth rates during the period. The hydro power is the major industry of the country. The industrial development in Maldives is at a lower level in comparison to other relatively industrially advanced countries of the region like India, Sri Lanka and Pakistan. In this country, during 1991-97, the annual growth rate averaged at 8.6 per cent, which was higher than 6.6 per cent, recorded during 1980s. Nepal being in the same category as Maldives, also has an underdeveloped industrial structure. It registered an average growth rate (8 per cent) during 1991-97 that was lower than 9 per cent registered during 1990s. In 1994-97, the mean growth rate was 5.5 per cent with low fluctuation (C.V. 0.47). The prominent industries here include woolen carpets, readymade garments, cotton textiles and jute goods.

TABLE-2.3

Growth performance of Industrial Sector in SAARC countries

(Per cent per annum)

Region/ Country	Ave. 1981-90	Ave. 1991-97	1994	1995	1996	1997	Ave. 1994-97	S.D. 1994-97	C.V. 94-97
SAARC	5.7	6.5	8.6	12.2	6.5	5.5	8.2	2.96	0.36
Bangladesh	7.1	6.4	7.8	8.4	5.3	3.6	6.3	2.22	0.35
Bhutan	9.9	9.4	13.9	17.0	8.4	1.6	10.2	6.76	0.66
India	5.4	6.6	9.4	14.1	7.2	6.0	9.2	3.57	0.39
Maldives	6.6	8.6	6.6	8.2	—	—	—	—	—
Nepal	9.0	8.0	9.0	3.9	5.9	3.2	5.5	2.60	0.47
Pakistan	5.9	5.2	4.5	4.8	3.6	3.3	4.1	0.71	0.17
Sri Lanka	7.4	7.2	8.1	7.8	5.6	7.9	7.4	1.17	0.16

Source: ADB—Asian Development Outlook: various issues.

In Pakistan, the average annual growth rate of industry declined to 5.2 per cent during the period 1991-97 from 5.9 per cent in 1980s. The Pakistani industrial sector has persistently experienced the recession in 1990s, recording the lowest average annual growth rate in the region. On calculating the mean growth rate for the period 1994-97, it further declined to 4.1 per cent with comparatively very low variability as the C.V. for the period was 0.17. Sri Lanka registered an average annual growth rate of 7.4 per cent for its industrial sector during 1980s, which is marginally up from the mean growth rate of 7.2 per cent recorded during 1991-97. Major industries of the country are agro-based including food processing, beverages, tobacco and textiles. Sri Lanka has relatively diversified industrial structure. For 1994-97, the average was 7.4 with C.V. of 0.16.

In India, the industrial sector grew with annual average growth rates of 5.4 per cent during 1980s and 6.6 per cent during 1991-97. During 1994-97, the annual growth rate of the sector jumped to 9.2 per cent with C.V. being 0.39. It was the cumulative result of many path-breaking initiatives taken in the industrial sector in particular and economy in general. At the industrial level, they mainly comprised deregulation and delicensing of industrial sector, rationalisation and reduction of import duties and lowering down of corporate taxes. At the macro economy level, they included containing the fiscal deficit, reduction in overall interest rates, switching over to market-determined exchange rate, extending rupee convertibility to current account, etc.[10] All these measures were to lead the economy to a low cost and efficient regime.

Services Sector

Services sector is the most prominent among all three sectors in the SAARC countries, contributing over 40 per cent to GDP of the region as a whole. Its performance has improved during 1990s over the previous decade. It registered an average annual growth rate of 5.7 per cent during 1980s, which scaled up to 6.9

per cent during 1991-97. On reckoning for the period 1994-97, the average is still higher at 7.7 per cent with very low fluctuation as C.V. being 0.12 for the period. However, major part of the services in the region comes from tourism-related activities and low level services, albeit India has recently earned a good name in the software-related services the world- over. Table 2.4 shows the performance of each individual country of the region in the services sector during the last two decades.

In Bangladesh, the average growth rate of the sector during the period 1991-97 was 5.7 per cent per annum, compared to 5.3 per cent recorded in 1980s. During 1994-97,the average growth rate further improved to 6.4 per cent with comparatively low variability, the C.V. being 0.07. In Bhutan, the services sector's annual average growth rate increased to 7.4 per cent during 1991-97 from 6.1 per cent registered in the previous decade of 1980s. During 1994-97, the average growth rate improved marginally to 7.8 per cent. It experienced relatively high level of variation in its growth rates for the period 1994-97, C.V. being 0.52.

The average annual growth rates of the sector in India were 5.9 per cent during 1980s and 7.3 per cent during the period 1991-97. The mean growth rate further increased to 8.4 per cent when calculated for the period 1994-97 with comparatively low year-to-year fluctuation (C.V. 0.14). Maldives' services sector contribution to GDP is the highest in the SAARC region. It was above 60 per cent in 1997. The sector grew with the average annual rates of 6.5 per cent during 1981-90 and 8.2 per cent during 1991-97. Its services sector's average growth rate was the highest in South Asia during 1991-97. The high growth of the services sector is due to sharp rise in the growth performance of the tourism sector in the country.

In Nepal, growth rates of the services sector averaged at 7.2 per cent for both the periods, 1980s and 1991-97. The average slightly declined to 6.7 per cent during 1994-97. However, the year-to-year fluctuation was low as the Coefficient

TABLE-2.4

Growth Performance of Services Sector in SAARC Countries

(Per cent per annum)

Region/ Country	Ave. 1981-90	Ave. 1991-97	1994	1995	1996	1997	Ave. 1994-97	S.D. 1994-97	C.V. 94-97
SAARC	5.7	6.9	6.9	8.8	6.9	8.1	7.7	0.94	0.12
Bangladesh	5.3	5.7	5.8	6.9	6.5	6.2	6.35	0.47	0.07
Bhutan	6.1	7.4	6.2	5.9	5.2	13.9	7.8	4.1	0.52
India	5.9	7.3	7.5	9.8	7.3	9.1	8.4	1.2	0.14
Maldives	6.5	8.2	8.1	8.7	—	—	—	—	—
Nepal	7.2	7.2	7.7	6.0	7.9	5.0	6.7	1.4	0.21
Pakistan	4.9	4.9	4.2	4.8	4.7	4.1	4.5	0.35	0.07
Sri Lanka	5.6	5.6	5.1	4.9	6.0	5.6	5.4	0.50	0.09

Source: ADB—Asian Development Outlook: various issues.

of Variation (C.V.) was calculated at 0.21 for the period. The services sector in Pakistan performed poorly as compared to the average of the SAARC region during almost the last one and a half decades. It secured the average annual growth rate of 4.9 per cent during 1981-97. During 1994-97, it had the annual growth rate of 4.5 per cent with C.V. being 0.07. Sri Lanka's services sector registered the mean annual growth rate of 5.6 per cent throughout the period 1981-97. The average for the period 1994-97 was 5.4 per cent with low year-to-year fluctuation, C.V. being 0.09 for the period.

Intra-Regional Trade

To analyse the trade performance among the countries of the region before the conclusion of SAARC Preferential Trading Arrangement in 1995, the trade turnover in four different years, 1980, 1985, 1990 and 1996, have been studied. Tables 2.5 and 2.6 show the export and import volumes in four different years among the SAARC countries as well as within the SAARC region as a whole.

It is clear from the Tables 2.5 and 2.6 that the trade volume within the region has increased over the four different years taken for the analysis. However, as a percentage of total imports and exports to the world, a grim picture emerges. The export volume within the region has increased from mere $640 million in 1980 to $2105 million in year 1996, while as a percentage of the total exports of the region to the world, it has declined from 4.9 per cent to 4.2 per cent respectively for the same period. The import volume within the region has almost quadrupled over the period 1980-1996 from $603 million in 1980 to $2491 million in 1996. However, as a percentage of the total imports of the region from the world, it declined to 1.9 per cent in 1990 from 2.4 per cent in 1980 and then increased to 4.1 per cent in 1996. It indicates that the trade volume of the SAARC countries grew slower within the region than trade turnover with the world.

TABLE- 2.5

Intra- SAARC Trade—1980-1996

(In million dollars)

Country / Year	Bangladesh				Bhutan				India				Nepal				Maldives				Pakistan				Sri Lanka			
	80	**85**	**90**	**96**	**80**	**85**	**90**	**96**	**80**	**85**	**90**	**96**	**80**	**85**	**90**	**96**	**80**	**85**	**90**	**96**	**80**	**85**	**90**	**96**	**80**	**85**	**90**	**96**
Exports																												
Bangladesh	—	—	—	—	—	—	—	—	8	30	22	21	0.5	5.1	7	1	—	0.1	—	—	55	42	23	37	5	0.2	8	2
India	106	59	297	832	—	—	—	15	—	—	—	—	95	83	40	158	3	1	5	15	2	14	43	141	101	68	102	458
Maldives	—	—	—	—	—	—	—	—	—	—	—	—	—	—	—	—	—	—	—	—	0.4	—	—	25	1.7	4.1	7	1.3
Nepal	0.9	—	–1	5	—	—	—	—	19	40	14	33	—	—	—	—	—	—	—	—	3.6	1.8	—	—	0.4	4	—	—
Pakistan	55	65	103	109	—	—	—	–1	71	38	49	41	0.1	0.1	1	6	0.3	0.3	1	3	—	—	—	—	39	42	69	80
Sri Lanka	4	15	10	12	—	—	—	—	34	6	20	43	—	0.1	—	1	1.2	5.2	7	16	34	27	32	37	—	—	—	—
Imports																												
Bangladesh	—	—	—	—	—	—	7	4	56	65	170	1018	1	—	2	6	—	—	—	—	35	18	70	90	4.7	4.8	8	10
India	12	33	15	58	—	—	—	—	—	—	—	—	21	44	15	49	—	—	—	—	76	41	45	39	32	7	22	35
Maldives	—	0.1	—	—	—	—	—	—	3.2	0.4	7	36	—	—	—	—	—	—	—	—	0.2	0.3	1	3	1.3	5.7	10	18
Nepal	0.5	5.6	8	1	—	—	—	—	104	91	43	150	—	—	—	—	—	—	—	—	0.4	0.1	1	6	—	—	—	0.1
Pakistan	76	46	36	86	—	—	—	—	3.9	16	46	212	4	2	—	—	0.5	0.1	—	27	—	—	—	—	40	31	37	45
Sri Lanka	3	0.2	9	2	—	—	—	—	96	75	118	562	0.4	4.4	—	—	1.9	4.3	6	17	30	34	51	69	—	—	—	—

Source: IMF: Direction of Trade Statistics: Various Annual Issues.

TABLE-2.6

Total Exports and Imports within SAARC Region

(In million dollars)

Country / Year	Total % of total Export to World				Total % of total Imports to World			
	1980	**1985**	**1990**	**1996**	**1980**	**1985**	**1990**	**1996**
Bangladesh	68.5 (8.7)	77.4 (7.7)	60 (3.5)	61 (1.9)	96.7 (3.7)	87.8 (3.5)	257 (7.03)	1124 (16.3)
India	307 (3.6)	22 (2.2)	487 (2.7)	1619 (5.01)	141 (0.9)	125 (0.7)	97 (0.4)	181 (0.5)
Maldives	2.1 (26.2)	4.1 (17)	7 (13.4)	38 (29.5)	4.7 (23)	6.5 (9.1)	18 (13)	57 (13.5)
Nepal	23.9 (37.8)	45.8 (33.6)	15 (6.9)	38 (11)	104.9 (47.8)	96.7 (33)	52 (11.5)	158 (24.5)
Pakistan	165.7 (6.3)	145.4 (5.3)	223 (4)	240 (260)	124.5 (2.3)	95.1 (1.6)	121 (1.6)	320 (2.6)
Sri Lanka	73.2 (7)	53.3 (4.2)	59 (3.6)	109 (2.7)	131.3 (6.5)	117.9 (6.4)	184 (6.9)	647 (12.9)
Grand Total	**640** **(4.9)**	**551** **(3.6)**	**861** **(3.16)**	**2105** **(4.2)**	**603** **(2.4)**	**529** **(1.9)**	**729** **(1.9)**	**2491** **(4.1)**

Source: IMF—Direction of Trade Statistics: Various Annual Issues.

Studying individually each SAARC country, the scene is almost the same. The export and import volumes have increased for all the countries over the period 1980-96, but as a percentage of their total global exports and imports, they have declined. Only India and Maldives were able to increase the proportion of their total world exports going to the SAARC region over 1980-96, while the remaining–Bangladesh, Pakistan, Nepal and Sri Lanka–registered a decline. Maldives tops the SAARC states in terms of its exports to the region as a percentage of its total world exports by securing 29.5 per cent, followed by Nepal (11 per cent), India (5.01 per cent), Sri Lanka (2.7 per cent), Pakistan (2.6 per cent) and Bangladesh (1.9 per cent) in 1996. The share of imports from SAARC region in the total imports of SAARC countries from world in 1996 stood at 24.50 per cent, 16.3 per cent, 12.9 per cent, 13.5 per cent, 2.6 per cent and 0.5 per cent in the case of Nepal, Bangladesh, Sri Lanka, Maldives, Pakistan and India respectively. For the whole SAARC region, it has increased from 2.4 per cent in 1980 to 4.1 per cent in 1996.

The reasons for the poor trade flow among the SAARC countries can be broadly divided into two categories–structural and policy-induced reasons. The structural constraints stem from the fact that the patterns of production of the countries of the region are more or less the same because of their almost same latitudinal positions as well as their developmental stages being at the broad category of developing economies in the continuum scale of economic evolution. They lie within the same latitudes limiting their agricultural activities because of the similar climatic conditions except in case of different terrains. For example, Nepal and Bhutan have the mountainous terrain, whereas the Sri Lanka and Maldives being islands have mainly coastal areas. In industrial sector also, they have similar production baskets comprising the agro-based products, primary products and consumer products involving low technology.

Among the policy-induced reasons for the dismal trade performance within the region are pursuance of the import substitution policies to become self-reliant, lack of awareness about each other's tradable products, absence of an institutional mechanism to facilitate trade among them until SAPTA came into being in 1995, the lack of export capabilities in the region and political considerations, which generally ran against any economic cooperation.

All these factors require more elaboration. The import substitution policies widely adopted by the countries of the region until recently, in fact, led them to become the substitute economies rather than the complementary ones to each other. These policies also limited the market for the entrepreneurs of the region as high tariff and non-tariff barriers were used to protect the respective economies from outside competition. This, in turn, denied the benefit of economies of scale, economies of scope and specialisation to the entrepreneurs of the region, thus making their commodities uncompetitive on the price and quality fronts vis-à-vis their competitors from outside the region. This acted as a disincentive to big investments in the region, thereby undermining their export capabilities. Because of the small size of their markets, their GDPs were also below their potential, which reduced the overall saving and investment rates in the region.

The absence of institutional mechanism until SAPTA came into force was also an important reason for the slow progress of trade among the SAARC countries. Though economic cooperation is an important constituent of the SAARC Charter, no focussed attention was paid until the initiation of the regional trading bloc in the region in 1995. As a result, there was lack of compilation of data on the importable and exportable items besides the total absence of any incentive to export within the region. As far as petty political considerations are concerned, these generally prevailed over the economic sense, which proved to be anti-growth for the region. Such considerations encouraged these countries to adopt anti-trade, even disciminatory policies. Sometimes their decisions were biased in favour of sourcing the imports from outside the region while the better products were available within the region at competitive prices. All this was detrimental to the progress of the region. Because of all these reasons discussed above, there has not been any serious attempt to integrate the production capacities of the region vertically and horizontally. Now with the starting of the regional integration scheme under the regional trading bloc in the region, a proper combining of the production, marketing and export capabilities can be charted out in future.

References

1. World Bank, World Development Indicators, 1998.
2. ADB, *Asia Development Outlook 1998*; and ESCAP, *Economic and Social Survey of Asia and Pacific 1998*, United Nations.
3. Panandiker, V.A. Pai, "Problems of Governance and Agenda for South Asia", in V.A. Pai Panandiker (ed.), *"Problems of Governance in South Asia"*, (New Delhi, Konark Publishers Pvt. Ltd.), p.454.
4. UNDP: *Human Development Report, 1994*, Tables 21 and 51.
5. *SAARC Survey of Development and Cooperation 1998/99- RIS for the Non-Aligned and Other Developing Countries*, pp. 132-34.
6. Asia Development Outlook, 1997 and 98 Issues.
7. *Asia Development Outlook*, 97 and 98.
8. UNCTAD, *World Investment Reports* (1999).
9. IMF, *International Financial Statistics*, May 1998.
10. *Economic Survey of India* (Government of India): various Issues.

3

Regionalism versus Multilateralism

Regional Trading Blocs (RTBs), which were earlier allowed under General Agreement on Tariff and Trade (GATT), have also been recognized under World Trade Organization (WTO), the successor of GATT. Article XXIV of WTO, which came into force in 1995, has provisions regarding regional trading blocs.[1] Under such blocs, two or more countries come together and agree to transact the goods on the preferential terms and conditions in regard to the tariff and non-tariff barriers. Many such groupings have emerged over the years. Some prominent ones among them include European Union, North American Free Trade Agreement, Latin American Free Trade Association, Caribbean common market, Economic Community of Central African States, Gulf Cooperation Council, Association of South East Asian Nations, Asia Pacific Economic Cooperation and many others. The contemporary map of the world is littered with them. If one throws a dart at a map of the world, the probability is almost one hundred per cent that it will land on some trading bloc or the other. The South Asian region recognised the importance of a RTB very late and jumped on this bandwagon. It did not have an economic integration scheme under the regional trading bloc until recently when the initiative was taken with the establishment of SAPTA–SAARC Preferential trade Agreement in 1995, with its secretariat in Kathmandu, Nepal.

Economic Rationale of Opening up Regional Trading Blocs

The regional trading blocs have always evoked controversies. In fact, some of the economists are of the view that such regional groupings are against the MFN—Most Favoured Nation-clause, the soul of the whole philosophy of WTO.[2] Their contention is that under a RTB, member countries are given preferential treatment in terms of the tariff and non-tariff barriers for the purpose of imports. Thus, in a way, the non-member countries are discriminated in relation to those which are members. While under WTO, the MFN principle requires that a member of GATT extend to every other GATT member the same treatment meted out to the country that is the most favoured. Discrimination between GATT members is not allowed. So, they cite regional groupings as against the MFN clause of WTO. However, they are allowed under the WTO with the aim of furthering the process of dismantling the trade distorting barriers—tariff and non-tariffs, so as to unify the world economy into a single whole, which is the ultimate goal of WTO. There are two exceptions where the violation to MFN clause of WTO is allowed. In addition to the regional trading blocs, the differential treatment can also be accorded to the developing and least developed countries under WTO.

Article XXIV imposes two conditions on a trading bloc. The first is that trade restrictions among countries forming the bloc must be eliminated over a period, normally not exceeding 10 years. They can not be reimposed later. The purpose of this condition is to ensure that a trading bloc is not used to merely circumvent the MFN clause.

The second requirement, which is equally important, is that the common external tariffs levied after forming the bloc must not be higher than the average level of tariffs that existed in the member countries before the bloc was formed. It is the second requirement that is of primary interest to countries that are not members of the regional bloc. An example would make the idea more clear. Suppose there are three countries, X, Y, and Z. Prior to the formation of bloc, X imposes a tariff of 15 per cent on imports originating from the rest two countries, Y and Z. Likewise, Y imposes the tariff of 20 per cent on imports from X and Z. X and Y now decide to form a trading bloc and impose a common external tariff on imports from Z. As per the second requirement, this common external tariff cannot be higher than the weighted average of 15 per cent and 20 per cent. Although the second requirement for setting up a RTB has been expressed in the above example in terms of tariffs, it is equally applicable to all trade restrictions including non-tariff barriers as well. However, with the average tariffs continually declining, the old importance of tariffs is no longer there, and non-tariff barriers are extremely difficult to pinpoint. It is for these reasons that the second requirement has very little operational significance.[3]

During the Uruguay round of negotiations, a suggestion to include the third condition for establishing a regional trading bloc was made. This related to the continuous acceptance of new members into the union, so that trading blocs indeed become a stepping stone towards global free trade. However, it was not accepted.

Now-a-days most of the countries are opening up their economies at two levels—one, at the multi-lateral level under WTO, and two, at the regional level under a regional arrangement. The opening up is faster and deeper at the regional level so as to give preferential treatment to member countries.

The world is moving progressively towards a frictionless and seamless world economy, where all custom barriers will be withdrawn over a time-frame. This process, which was already on ever since the GATT came into force in 1948, has been intensified after the conclusion of the Uruguay Round of GATT Negotiations. This Round established the World Trade Organization (WTO), a formal institution with its Secretariat in Geneva, to facilitate the negotiations among the member countries to meet the above-mentioned goal of free movement of goods across the member countries.[4] The WTO also monitors the implementation of the agreements entered into by the members of WTO. If any member does not comply with the agreed commitments and pursues the policies inconsistent with WTO provisions, and the WTO receives a request from another member affected by such action, it has mechanism in the form of

Dispute Settlement Body (DSB) to force, that member to withdraw such WTO incompatible policies.[5]

Earlier it were only merchandise goods that were negotiated to be transacted at the reduced rate of tariffs under GATT. Of course, the non-tariff barriers were also negotiable. However, under WTO, not only merchandise goods but also services and investment are being negotiated for the free movement across the member countries. The services have been already included in the Uruguay Round under General Agreement on Trade in Services (GATS). This agreement is still incomplete. It is an open-ended agreement pursuing the bottom-to-top approach. Under this approach, every member country identifies the areas of services as per its comparative advantages and negotiates them with other member countries of WTO for opening up on a *quid-pro-quo* basis. The second round of negotiations on services is going on in Geneva.

As far as the agreement on investment is concerned, no comprehensive agreement has been reached so far, albeit some part of it is covered under GATS. In fact, it was one of the agenda items in the Seattle Meet conducted for the finalisation of items to be taken up for further negotiations. However, because of the failure of the Seattle Meet on account of dominance of disagreements over agreements on the issues among the member countries, no further negotiations have yet begun, albeit negotiations on agriculture and services, which are mandated negotiations, have already started in Geneva. Hence, the issue of agreement on investment has been shelved for the time being. This issue will finally crop up whenever the member countries agree for further negotiations.

The other issues, which were included for the first time for negotiations under the GATT, are Agreement on Textile and Clothing, under which textile and clothing have to be merged with the mainstream of trade by dismantling Multi-Fibre Arrangement (MFA) by 2005, and Agreement on Agriculture (AOA).[6] Under the AOA, the member countries of WTO have agreed to unshackle the agriculture sector from the multiple trade-distorting measures including domestic support to producers through subsidies, export subsidies and restrictions on imports through the tariff and non-tariff barriers.

The world is moving rapidly towards the free movement of goods and services. Investment too is also expected to freely move from one country to another in the near future. This system is going to stay on, based as it is on a sound economic logic. The strongest justification for this system is that it increases the welfare at the world level. The basic economic principle is that when two countries are engaged in trade, they are better off than when they do not go for trade. This principle is based on the comparative advantages of the countries involved in trade.[7] It implies that if the two countries, instead of attempting to produce all the goods needed by their respective societies themselves, only adopt those patterns of production where they have comparative advantages, and exchange the other goods from each other, their respective economies would gain as a whole. The consumers would get cheaper goods and the producers would enjoy the competitive edge through the economies of scale, specialisation and employment of better technology. The same argument can be applied at the world level also involving all the countries of the world. The world as a whole would gain if it gradually moves towards free trade, minimising the adverse impact of such opening up through giving sufficient time span for adjustments especially to developing and least developed economies and safety-nets for those adversely affected by such actions in the short-run. In fact, such problems are more profound in the developing countries because the LDCs have been kept out of many obligations under WTO. The developing countries' main problem emanates from the fact that there would be more layoffs in these countries due to relocation of industries as per their comparative advantages. They already have high unemployment rates. This relocation of industries might aggravate the problem and cause unrest in these countries. Hence they require sufficient time for such adjustments, albeit they have already been given more time to carry out their obligations under WTO vis-a-vis developed countries. Besides, they need financial and technical help for such relocation and to provide safety-nets to the vulnerable sections of their societies. The WTO does not have any provision for such assistance. A coordination among the various multilateral institutions, like World Bank, IMF and WTO, can be forged along with some negotiations with the developed countries under WTO for such help to the developing countries.

The other strong reason for staying in WTO-system is that if any country opts to be out of the system, it will have to make bilateral agreements with each and every country of the world. In that case, there are more chances of exploitation of the developing and least developed countries by the developed ones, whereas, in the present arrangement, the least developed states are exempted from most of the obligations of WTO, and the developing countries too have been given fairly equitable chances to negotiate. Moreover, the developing countries as a whole can collectively put pressure for carrying their demand through, though their interests are so diverse that they rarely make a combined move. They are also susceptible to lures and pressures from the developed countries. But still, they can forge partnerships on the basis of issues of their common interests. Further, the WTO has an in-built dispute settlement mechanism. If any country feels that it is being subjected to arm-twisting by any developed country in the matter of trade or any other matter related to WTO agreements, it can approach the WTO's Dispute Settlement Body (DSB) and get redressal of its grievances. DSB is flooded with many complaints ever since its inception, many of which have been lodged by the developing countries against their developed counterparts. Thus, the present system of WTO is far better for the developing countries than a *laissez faire* system, where every country exercises its might to gain through bilateral agreements. Under the present system, clouts can be used only at the time of negotiation of agreements, and once the agreements are concluded, they are binding on members for all times except in some special cases. Thus, the present system is more just and is based on codified rules and regulations with judicial power vested in DSB of WTO. The WTO is like a constitution of international trade, stating rights and obligations of every member country.

The rationale and benefits of regional trading blocs (RTBs) are the same as those at the world level under WTO. They also increase the welfare of the member countries both in the dynamic as well as static conditions. The welfare gains are more in a dynamic state accruing in the long term rather than in a static state in the short term. In the static state, the member countries of a bloc would be immediately benefited through trade creation. Trade creation implies that the country has replaced the expensive (domestic) supply by the cheaper (partner country) imports. *Ceteris Paribus*, it produces a welfare gain by providing the consumers with cheaper goods. In the dynamic situation, the gains multiply, as the countries of the bloc switch over to those patterns of production where they have comparative advantages. They would now experience the economies of scale, and over the period, they would acquire the specialisation in their respective production baskets. It would not only help the countries of the bloc in increasing their trade within the bloc but also sharpen their competitive edge in the world market outside the bloc. It would also add to their gains. In the dynamic state, the saving rates in these countries would also increase, as the consumers of these member countries of the bloc are getting cheaper goods and producers earning more profits due to the economies of scale and specialisation. This increased saving rate would help step up investments in these economies. The entrepreneurs from the outside bloc would also have an extra incentive to establish their production facilities within the bloc to avoid the common tariff and non-tariff barriers. Thus, the overall gains in the dynamic conditions far exceed the gains in the static state.

The central concepts of RTB's theory introduced by the Canadian economist Jacob Viner (1892-1970), are trade creation and trade diversion.[8] Trade creation occurs when a country starts importing a cheaper commodity that it previously produced at home before the formation of the bloc, while trade diversion takes place when a country starts to import an expensive commodity from a partner country after the bloc formation that it previously imported from the outside world. The concepts can be illustrated in the simplest Ricardian model with constant opportunity costs. To understand these concepts, we suppose three countries U, V and W. Consider U's trade in a particular commodity with production cost equal to Cu in U, Cv in V and Cw in W. Prior to the formation of the free trade area, country U's supply would come from whichever country had the minimum cost to the consumers:

$$C_u; (1 + T)\ C_v; (1 + T)\ C_w$$

where T is the tariff rate. On the formation of the free trade area between U and V, the tariff on imports from V is withdrawn. In this new situation also, the supply would come from the country that has the minimum cost to consumers.

$$C_u; C_v; (1+T)\ C_w$$

Since the cost of buying from the partner country (V) falls in the new scenario and the cost of buying from other two sources (U and W) remains constant, imports from V may be stimulated if

$$(1+ T)\ C_v > C_u > C_v$$

If the country previously produced the goods itself rather than importing from W, then in the new situation it will cease domestic production and import instead from its partner V. This is the trade creation.

If, on the other hand,

$$(1+T)\ C_w > C_v > C_w$$

and the country previously imported from W rather than producing the goods itself, then in the new situation it will buy from V instead of W. This is trade diversion. These concepts are, however, in no way restricted to the Ricardian constant cost model. Trade expansion with the partner country will still be trade creation so long as it involves an expansion in the total level of trade, and it will still be trade diversion when it involves the redirection of trade from third countries, even if the industries involved face increasing costs due to factor substitution or decreasing costs due to increasing returns of scale, or if they are imperfectly competitive.

Trade diversion in case of Custom Union is harmful, where the member countries adopt common tariffs based on weighted average tariffs in these countries. It implies that the country has replaced cheap imports from the outside world by expensive imports from its new partner.

As has been stated earlier, most of the countries are presently opening up their economies at two fronts–under WTO and regional arrangements. The opening up is faster and deeper at the regional level so as to give more benefits to the member countries of regional trading blocs (RTBs). Although there are two conditions for establishing RTBs specified in Article XXIV of WTO, it still leaves ample opportunities for manipulations so as to give extra benefits to the member countries at the expense of non-member countries. The second condition is related to the present context. As per this condition, the external tariffs set after forming the bloc must not be higher than the weighted average level of tariffs that existed in the member countries before the bloc was formed. In this way, it sets only the maximum limit of the weighted average common external tariff, and that too of a fixed nature. It leaves much scope for the benefits to the member countries of the bloc at the expense of non-member countries.

The second condition only talks about the custom union, where common external custom tariffs are used by each member country of the bloc and goods are imported within the bloc at the zero rate of tariff. The common external tariffs are fixed at the starting time of custom union. It simply means that if the tariff rates were at high levels in the member countries at the time of inception of the custom union the common external tariff rates would also be high. This situation might cause a lot of trade diversion for the non-member countries. Thus, they might get marginalised in these custom unions. However, the average tariff rates in general are coming down under multilateral agreements of WTO.

Moreover, the second condition talks about only common weighted average tariff rates for non-members, leaving lot of scope for manipulation by the member countries of custom Union through tariff peaks. Tariff peaks mean keeping higher external tariffs for those items where it might be beneficial for the member countries, thereby marginalising the non-member countries in these items.

The second condition for RTBs only takes into account the custom union, which comes generally second in the hierarchical stages of evolution of a RTB. It does not consider the first stage, which is 'Free Trade Zone'. Under this stage, a group of countries gets together and decides to remove all barriers to trade (tariffs as well as non-tariffs) among themselves. The individual countries are free to decide how trade will be conducted with the countries that are not members of the bloc. For example, independent tariffs can be set with non-member countries. It also does not speak about the pre-first stage of a RTB. This is called 'Preferential Trading Arrangement'. Under this stage, the member countries identify the commodities themselves to be transacted at the preferential terms and conditions in the form of tariff and non-tariff concessions. They negotiate step by step, bringing progressively the increasing number of items under the ambit of concessional regime. The SPATA is the example of this stage.

The silence of Article XXIV of WTO in the above mentioned two stages in the evolution of RTBs gives ample scope for manipulation by these blocs in favour of their member states. They can give very deep concessions to the member countries at these two stages without worrying about the external tariffs applicable to non-members. The second condition applies after entering into the custom union. That too is very mild in the form of maximum weighted average external common tariff at the starting time of custom union, giving opportunities for manipulation in the form of peak tariffs to benefit member countries at the cost of non-member countries. The discrimination might be effected till the ultimate goal of WTO to make the world economy seamless and frictionless is attained, which seems to be unforeseeable even in the distant future.

In the above analysis, we have only taken manipulation in favour of member countries of the bloc in regard to tariffs only. The Non-Tariff Barriers (NTBs) are other areas where similar manipulations can be effected to give more benefits to member countries of a RTB. In February 2000, the Indian Ministry of Commerce convened a meeting of the industry associations including ASSOCHAM, FICCI and CII. In that meeting, the issue of diversion of trade of the developing countries, especially India, in the strong regional blocs, like NAFTA and EU, was discussed threadbare. Although the Ministry did not come out with a list of specific items adversely affected due to trade diversion in these blocs, it cited the textile and clothing as one of the most potential items in NAFTA to get negatively affected especially after the total phasing out of the Multi-Fibre Arrangement (MFA) in 1995. It expressed the fears that India might lose its market to Mexico in the American and Canadian markets because of the tariff and non-tariff concessions given to Mexico under NAFTA. The Ministry asked the Industry Associations to prepare the comprehensive list of the items that are already being adversely impacted or which are potentially vulnerable.

Thus, the corollary of the above given analysis is that the countries which belong to the strong regional trading blocs with substantial intra-bloc trade are at the advantageous position *vis-a-vis* those countries belonging to weak regional blocs with insignificant intra-bloc trade or having no membership of any bloc. The member states of a strong regional trading bloc will be able to meet the major part of their import needs within the bloc through substantial trade creation by giving tariff and non-tariff concessions to its members, thereby driving out their close competitors from the bloc. The countries having no membership of any bloc or affiliated to weak ones with negligible intra-bloc trade might lose their markets in these strong regional blocs, while their import needs are still being satisfied from the outside blocs. It means that their exports are getting adversely affected in the strong regional blocs, while their imports are of the same level in the static situation and increasing over the period with the economic growth of these countries. This, in turn, is deteriorating the trade balance of these countries, thereby worsening their overall balance of payment position.

Regional Trading Blocs: Stages of Evolution

Looking into the theoretical stages of the evolution of a regional trading bloc, they can be categorised into five stages if the Preferential Trading Arrangement is taken as the first stage. In most books, four stages of evolution have been given. However, in practice, generally a RTB starts with Preferential Trading Arrangement. Hence, we have taken it as the first stage of evolution of a RTB. Under this stage, as has been mentioned earlier, the member countries identify some items individually to be traded at concessional rate of tariffs. The concessions in non-tariff barriers might also be included in this stage. The SAPTA (South Asian Preferential Trade Agreement) is an example of the first stage.

The second stage is Free Trade Zone. Under this stage, the member countries abolish all restrictions to trade within the bloc among the member states.[9] The individual countries of the bloc are free to decide their own external trade policies. For instance, each country can set independent tariffs with non-member countries. The third stage, which goes beyond that of a free trade area, is Customs Union. Members of a customs union obviously have free trade among themselves. But, in addition, they decide on a common uniform commercial policy (tariffs and NTBs) for trade with non-members. Members of a customs union will, therefore, have the same tariff for imports from a country that is not a member of the customs union. The fourth stage of evolution of a regional trading bloc is Common Market. A common market allows free movement of labour and capital within the common market besides having the two features of customs union, namely, free trade among member countries and a uniform tariff policy towards non-members. The fifth and final stage is Economic Union. Apart from satisfying the conditions of the common market, the economic union achieves some degree of harmonisation of the economic policies of the member countries. These economic policies include monetary policy, fiscal policy, exchange rate policy, taxation policy, etc. They also attempt to adopt a single currency. European Economic Community (EEC) falls under this category.

In fact, the regional trading bloc is an attempt towards transforming economies of the member states of the bloc into a single unified economy. It can not be achieved in a short span of time. It starts with the easily pursued measures by the member states with establishing Preferential Trading Arrangement, and it ends with setting up Economic Union (EU). In between these two extreme points of stages of evolution of a RTB lie at least three stages, which require many hard measures by the member states and lot of painful adjustments in the economies. It takes quite a long time. The European Economic Community (EEC), also known as European Common Market, is by far the most successful of all regional economic integration schemes. This integration scheme comprising originally six nations, namely, Belgium, France, Germany, Italy, Luxembourg and Netherlands, was brought into being in January 1958 with the Treaty of Rome (1957). It took almost thirty-five years to become common market, second last stage of a regional economic integration scheme. By July 1968, it had established the customs union by abolishing tariff on trade among themselves and adopting the common tariff schedule on imports from other countries. The community members had also taken some noteworthy steps towards approximating their economic policies including adoption of Common Agriculture Policy (CAP) in 1962 and establishment of the European Monetary System in 1979. A detailed programme for attaining a single integrated market was set forth by the EC Commission (the EC's Executive Body) in June 1985 in a white paper entitled "Completing the Internal Market". The EC Council (the EC's Supreme decision making body) promptly entrusted EC to carry out the white paper programme by 1992.

The white paper listed 300 specific areas (subsequently reduced to 279) for actions by 1992. These actions were intended to eliminate the physical, technical and fiscal obstacles to an integrated market to achieve a genuine European Community without internal economic frontiers and with freedom of movement for goods, services, persons and capital. The barriers targeted for removal pertained to the following nine categories.

- Border Control
- Limitation on Movement of People.
- People's Right of Establishment
- Differing Internal Taxation Regimes
- Lack of Common Legal Framework for Business
- Controls on Movement of Capital
- Heavy and Differing Regulations of Services
- Divergent Product Regulations and Standards
- Protectionist Public Procurement Policies

The share of intra-regional trade in the total world trade increased in the 1980s in West Europe, North America and Asia. In other words, trade within the region grew substantially faster than the world trade. In 1990, intra-regional trade in goods accounted for 61 per cent of total trade in goods of the European Community. If the European Free Trade Area nations are included in the community, the ratio of intra-West European Trade could be about 70 per cent. The corresponding figures were 41 per cent for Asia and 35 per cent for North America. Over 60 per cent of trade of the Pacific Rim Nations stay within the area. Regional integration schemes tend to increase intra-regional trade. For instance, trade between the 12 members of the EC increased from about 40 per cent in 1960 to 60 per cent in 1990. The intra-regional trade has also increased in NAFTA and ASEAN.

Why Regional Blocs are more successful in Developed Countries

Empirical studies of regional trading blocs have suggested that the regional trading blocs among developed countries are more successful in creating intra-bloc trade in comparison to their counterparts among developing countries. The same studies also show that trade creation has predominated (by as much as 4 to 1 in the case of the EEC). A comparative study reveals that the levels of Intra-bloc trade were to the tune of 47.5 per cent and 62 per cent of the total exports in NAFTA and EU respectively in 1996, whereas it was just 4.3 per cent of total exports in the case of SAPTA .[10] The intra-bloc trade is also very low in the case of CARICOM (Caribbean Common Market) and West African Economic Community and many others among developing countries being less than 10 per cent of their total exports.

The reasons for it are not difficult to trace. In fact, it is mainly patterns of production of the developed and developing countries which make the difference. The developed countries are developed because they have moved up the stages of economic evolution in comparison to their developing counterparts. They have shifted to a more sophisticated pattern of production predominated by manufacturing industries involving very sophisticated technologies and knowledge-based services. In the industries involving advanced technologies, it is possible to produce a range of differentiated products in the same item. That is why these trading blocs (NAFTA, EU and ASEAN) were able to create trade to such an extent. For example, in automobile industry or knowledge-based industry (both hardware and software), it is possible to produce a range having different properties in the same items. Thus in spite of having similar patterns of production, they are able to specialise in some differentiated products.

If these blocs have some countries with developing economy's characteristics, it would further add to their advantages. In NAFTA, Mexico is a country having mainly labour-intensive industries.[11] It helps in creating more intra-regional trade. ASEAN also has a combination of countries that are at different stages of development. Myanmar is mainly an agriculture economy with agriculture contributing almost 60 per cent to its G.D.P. Philippines has maintained a balance among the industry, agriculture and service sectors. Singapore, Malaysia. Indonesia and Thailand are predominantly industrial countries. Thus, ASEAN is also a mixed bag of countries having different patterns of production, which enabled it to create substantial intra-bloc trade. It was 23 per cent of total exports of the group to the world in 1996

Analysing the position of the developing countries, we find that these countries are mainly agriculture-based economies. They have just moved to the industrialisation phase, and hence the industrial sector is at the nascent stage there. They have predominantly agro- based industries or labour-intensive industries employing low level of technologies. In these industries, the product differentiation becomes extremely difficult. This is true for the agriculture sector also. Since generally regional trading blocs are preferred among the contiguous states, they lie more or less on the same latitudinal positions having similar climatic conditions. This restricts production of varied agricultural items, and so they end up producing more or less similar items in agriculture sector also. Thus, the overall result is that they have similar patterns of production and lack complementarity. For the same reasons, in the international market too, they behave like competitors to each other. These are some of the reasons as to why attempts of economic integration schemes among developing countries could not produce perceptible results. Some economists believe (statistical evidence also confirms it) that in trade blocs among developing countries, trade diversions may have exceeded trade creation and member countries squabble bitterly about the distribution of new industry attracted by enlarged market. However, these conclusions can be challenged.

Countries on the road to industrialisation generally want to establish infant industries: their aim in forming a common market or free trade area is to provide a bigger market to permit them to establish and expand infant industries more rapidly and more cheaply than would otherwise be possible. In this case, the trade creation or trade diversion depends on whether the infant industries are established in one's own country or partner's country if the collective aim of the bloc is to promote import-substituting industrialisation. If the infant industry is established in one's own country, it is trade creation and if in partner's country, then it is trade diversion. But in real sense, it is trade diversion in both cases as consumers now pay higher prices for imports. However, the fact that trade diversion exceeds trade creation is not necessarily a sign of failure if the aim of the union is promotion of import substituting industries. It is, in fact, consistent with success. However, this success does not guarantee that all the members will be happy after the formation of a bloc. Even when it is collectively desired, trade diversion still involves a cost to the importer, who has to pay more. A member gains, in such cases, when the industries are established in its own country and loses when established in partner's country. No wonder they squabble over the location of new industries. However, this does not imply that the task they attempted was foolish. It just shows that it is inherently more difficult to maintain a balance, in case of a bloc among developing countries, from which all members could gain than it is when integration occurs among developed countries, each of which already has an advanced industrial structure. In latter case, the mutual gain can flow from increased intra-industry trade in differentiated products.

References

1. Bibek,Debroy, *Beyond the Uruguay Round: The Indian Perspective on GATT* (Response Book, New Delhi, 1996) p.23.
2. Muchkund Dubey, *An Unequal Treaty: World Trading Order After GATT,(*New Age International Limited, New Delhi,1996) p. 131.
3. Bibek,Debroy, *Beyond the Uruguay Round: The Indian Perspective on GATT,* (Response Book, New Delhi, 1996) p.24
4. Francis Cherunilam, "*International Business Environment", International Business,* (Wheller Publishing, New Delhi, 1998) p. 93.
5. Muchkund Dubey, *An Unequal Treaty: World Trading Order After GATT* (New Age International Publisher, New Delhi, 1996) pp. 90,91.
6. Bibek Debroy, *Beyond the Uruguay Round: The Indian Perspective on GATT,* (Response Book, New Delhi, 1996) p. 32.
7. John Williamson, *The Open Economy and The World Economy* (Basic Books, Inc., Publishers, New York) p. 25,26.
8. *Ibid.*,p. 95
9. Francis Cherunilam, "*International Business Environment*", *International Business,* (WhellerPublishing, New Delhi, 1998) p. 79.
10. *SAARC- Survey of Development and Cooperation 1998/99 (*Research and Information System for the Non-Aligned & other Developing Countries), p. 155
11. Steven Globeerman, "The Economics of NAFTA", in Alan M. Rugman (ed.), *Foreign Investment and NAFTA* (University of South Carolina Press, Columbia, 1994) pp.3-24.

4

Anatomy of SAARC Preferential Trade Agreement

The countries belonging to the strong regional blocs are at an advantageous position at the expense of countries having no affiliation to any bloc or belonging to the weak ones, as stated in the last chapter. The South Asian region lagged behind in terms of regional cooperation under the economic integration scheme in comparison to North America, Western Europe and South East Asia, and for that reason, countries of this region were at a disadvantageous position vis-à-vis their counterparts belonging to these strong regional blocs. In South Asia beginning in this regard was made with the establishment of SAPTA-SAARC Preferential Trade Agreement, finalised and signed in Dhaka in 1993. The Agreement was to enable the countries to enter the first round of trade negotiations to exchange trade preferences and concessions. The Agreement underlined the critical importance of promoting intra-regional cooperation, particularly in the field of manufactures, to enhance the productive capacity of the member countries. It also aimed at promoting the sustained economic growth and development to prevent the marginalisation of South Asia's trade interests in the larger context.

SAPTA is governed by the provisions of the Dhakha Agreement and also by the rules, regulations, decisions, understandings and protocols to be agreed upon within its framework by the Contracting States. SAPTA is to be governed in accordance with the following principles enshrined in the Agreement:[1]

- SAPTA shall be based on the principles of overall reciprocity and mutuality of advantages in such a way as to benefit equitably all Contracting States, taking into account their respective levels of economic and industrial development, the pattern of their external trade, trade and tariff policies and system;

- SAPTA shall be negotiated step by step and improved and extended in successive stages with periodic reviews;
- SAPTA shall recognise the special needs of the Least Developed Countries (LDCs) and provide the concrete preferential measures in their favour;
- SAPTA shall include all commodities in their raw, semi– processed and processed forms.

The principles of reciprocity and according special importance to the LDCs are of prime significance. Reciprocity implies serving the interests of all Contracting States, whereas special emphasis on LDCs (including Nepal, Bhutan, Maldives and Bangladesh) means allaying fears of the small states regarding major benefits of such cooperation accruing to the big states of the region, and their economies being swamped by the goods originating from them. The special importance attached to the LDCs might be in the form of more tariff and non- tariff concessions to imports from these states and assistance for developing their export capabilities by other relatively big states of the region. Articles 6 and 10 of the Agreement deal with the special emphasis on LDCs, which would be elaborately analysed in the latter part of this chapter.

Mechanism of Negotiation

Under SAPTA, the negotiations can be held in regard to tariff, para- tariff, non-tariff measures and direct trade measures. The Contracting States may conduct their negotiations for trade liberalisation through product-by-product basis, across-the-board tariffs reductions, sectoral basis and direct trade measures. They may choose any one of the above methods or any combination of them. The Contracting States have agreed to negotiate tariff preferences initially on a product-to- product basis. The

Contracting States have also agreed for trade facilitation and other measures to support and complement SAPTA for mutual benefits. As per Article 12, the Contracting States have agreed to undertake appropriate steps and measures for developing and improving the communication system, the transport infrastructure and the transit facilities for accelerating the growth of trade within the region.

Special Importance to LDCs

Special consideration shall be given to the requests from LDCs of the region for technical assistance and cooperation arrangements designed to assist them in expanding their trade with other Contracting States and in taking advantage of the potential benefits of SAPTA. These additional measures in favour of LDCs as per Article 6[2] of the Agreement might include-

- Helping the LDCs in identifying, preparing and establishing the industrial and agricultural projects on their territories to expand their export capabilities. They should be linked with buy- back arrangements.
- Setting up of manufacturing and other facilities in LDCs to meet intra-regional demand under co-operative arrangements.
- Formulation of export promotion policies and the establishment of training facilities in the field of trade to assist LDCs in expanding their exports and maximising their benefits from SAPTA.
- Provision of support to exports and marketing of products of LDCs by enabling these countries to share the existing facilities with the relatively big economies (for example, with respect to export credit insurance, access to market information, etc.) and by institutional and other positive measures to facilitate imports from LDCs in their own markets.

- Bringing together of enterprises in other Contracting States with project sponsors in the LDCs (both public and private) with a view to promoting joint ventures in projects designed to lead to the expansion of trade.
- Provision of special facilities and rates in respect to shipping.

Article 10 further spells out the provisions for special care for the LDCs by enjoining that 'in addition to other provisions of this Agreement, all Contracting States shall provide, wherever possible, special and more favourable treatment exclusively to the Least Developed Contracting States.'[3] These favourable treatments might include duty-free access, exclusive tariff preferences or deeper tariff preferences for the export products, the removal of non-tariff barriers and the removal, wherever appropriate, of para-tariff barriers. They further comprise the negotiations of long-term contracts with a view to assisting LDCs to achieve a reasonable level of sustainable exports of their products. Other such measures are, besides special consideration of exports from LDCs in application of safeguard measures, greater flexibility in the introduction and continuance of quantitative or other restrictions provisionally and without discrimination in critical circumstances by the LDCs.

It is clear from the above that the Agreement takes adequate care of the relatively less developed economies of the region. They have not only been given extra-market access through more concession in tariff, para-tariff and non-tariff barriers, but have also been assured of all technical as well as financial help in expanding their export potentialities. Sufficient provisions have been kept in the Agreement to ensure the equitable benefits of the regional co-operation to all, including LDCs. This has led to enthusiastic participation of the LDCs of the region in all the three rounds of negotiations held so far. The LDCs have even given concessions in tariff and non-tariff barriers on several items to other states of the region. However, in the three rounds of negotiations, the gains of the LDCs have remained confined to greater market access through deeper tariff and non-tariff concessions. No attempt has been made so far to strengthen their production bases and export capabilities. It is perhaps one of the main reasons for the low level of trade creation within SAPTA even after the lapse of almost five years since its coming into force in 1995. It was just 4.8 per cent of total exports of the region to the world in 1998- 99,[4] which is extremely low in comparison to other regional blocs, like NAFTA, EC, ASEAN, etc.

This issue was taken up intensively in the third meeting of The Inter-Governmental Group (IGG) on Trade Liberalization in SAARC Secretariat, Kathmandu. The delegates from the least developed countries reiterated that decisions taken in the earlier meetings of IGG on giving additional and more favourable treatment to their products, as also enunciated in the Articles 6 and 10 of the SAPTA Agreement, should be implemented and their products be given duty free access in the markets of other member states on a non-reciprocal basis. They also indicated that they would require technical assistance and training. Attention was drawn to the need of improving transport and transit facilities for the LDCs, two of which (Nepal and Bhutan) are land- locked. In this regard, the SAARC Technical Committee on Transport laid emphasis on early consideration of the SAARC Study on Transport Infrastructure and Transit Facilities in the region. The delegates from India, Pakistan and Sri Lanka on their part assured the LDCs more market access to their products in their respective economies and all possible technical assistance to develop their export capabilities and infrastructure. LDCs were also requested to identify the areas in which they require technical assistance and training so that appropriate steps could be taken.

Schedule of Concessions

The tariff, para-tariff and non-tariff concessions negotiated and exchanged amongst the Contracting States would be incorporated in the National Schedule of Concessions. These are negotiated separately with each member state of the region. The concessions agreed to under SAPTA, except those made exclusively to the least developed Contracting States in pursuance of Article 10 of this Agreement, would be extended unconditionally to all Contracting States. The commodities for concessions can also be offered by each country in a consolidated package called the 'Consolidated National Schedule of Concessions'. In the first round of negotiations, the 'Consolidated National Schedules of Concessions' were granted by all the Contracting States. In the second and the third rounds, both the methods were used.

Committee of Participants

As per Article 9 of the Agreement, a Committee of Participants has been established.[5] The Committee is supposed to meet at least once a year to review the progress made in the implementation of this Agreement. It will also ensure that the benefits of trade expansion emanating from this Agreement accrue to all Contracting States equitably. The Committee would also accord adequate opportunities for consultation on representations made by any Contracting State with respect to any matter affecting the implementation of the Agreement. The Committee would adopt appropriate measures for settling such representations. The Committee would determine its own rules of procedures.

The Committee would also work as the 'Dispute Settlement Body' to resolve the disputes on any matter related to the Agreement. As per Article 20, any dispute that may arise among the Contracting States regarding the interpretation and application of the provisions of this Agreement or any instrument adopted within its framework would be amicably settled by agreement between the parties concerned. In the event of failure to settle a dispute, a party to the dispute may refer it to the Committee. The Committee would review the matter and make the recommendation thereon within 120 days from the date on which the dispute was submitted to it. The Committee would adopt the appropriate rules for this purpose.

Whether the ruling of the Committee would be binding on the parties to the dispute is not clear from the Agreement. What action would be followed if the party to dispute against which the ruling has been pronounced does not accept it, is also not clear from the Agreement. This would be clear when such disputes would be brought to the Committee. The method adopted in World Trade Organization (WTO) in such cases might give some idea here. It is the retaliatory method, which is adopted in WTO. The retaliatory actions can be initiated by the aggrieved party against the undisciplined party to the dispute that does not follow the ruling of the Dispute Settlement Body (DSB) of WTO. The retaliatory measures might be in the form of restricting its market access in some items of prime importance by imposing tariff or non- tariff barriers.

Safeguard Measures

The Agreement also has some safeguard measures, which are available to every contracting state alike, to protect the interests of the states in the extra-ordinary circumstances, like balance of payment problem, massive damage to the domestic industries due to a sudden surge in imports of some products included in the national schedule of concessions, etc. These safeguards have been elaborated in Articles 13 and 14 of the Agreement[6]. These are:

- Notwithstanding the provisions of this Agreement, any Contracting State facing serious economic problems, including balance of payment difficulties, may suspend provisionally the concessions as to the quantity and the value of merchandise permitted to be imported under the Agreement. When such action is initiated, the Committee and the other Contracting States must be immediately notified of this action. It is obligatory on the part of state pursuing such action to provide, upon request from any other Contracting State, adequate opportunities for consultations with a view to preserving stability of the concessions negotiated under the SAPTA. If no satisfactory adjustment is effected between the Contracting States concerned within 90 days of such notification, the matter may be referred to the Committee for review.

- If any product, which is subject to a concession under this Agreement, is imported into the territory of a Contracting State in such a manner or in such quantities as to cause or threaten to cause serious injury to the domestic suppliers in that particular product, the importing state may, with prior consultations, suspend provisionally without discrimination the concessions accorded under the Agreement. When such action has taken place, the Contracting State that initiates such action would simultaneously notify the other Contracting States concerned and the Committee. The Committee would enter into consultations with the concerned Contracting State and endeavor to reach mutually acceptable agreement to remedy the situation. In the event of failure of the Contracting States to resolve the issue within 90 days of the receipt of original notification, the Committee of the Participants shall meet within 30 days to review the situation and try to settle the issue amicably. If the consultations in the Committee of Participants fail to resolve the issue within 60 days, the parties affected by such action shall have the right to withdraw equivalent concessions or other obligations that the Committee does not disapprove.

These safeguard measures have been provided to protect the Contracting States from the sudden adverse impact on their economies due to the implementation of the Agreement. This adverse impact might be in the form of severely worsened balance of payment position or major injury to the domestic suppliers in any specific item. Under the former case arising on account of balance of payment problem, the concerned state might provisionally suspend all the concessions on all items or some items under the Agreement. After 90 days, if no proper solution acceptable to all states concerned is found, the matter will be referred to the Committee for review. If the Committee does not find the justifiable ground for such suspension of the concessions, it might ask for the restoration of the concessions agreed earlier under the Agreement. Thus the minimum 90 days for such suspension of concessions have been given in the Agreement. The time period for review the Committee has not been specified in the Agreement.

In latter situation arising out of a sudden increase of imports of an item enlisted in the preferential list under the Agreement, causing massive injury to the domestic suppliers in that particular item, the importing state can suspend the concessions on that product for the maximum period of 180 days. After this limit, if an amicable solution accepted to all states concerned does not come through, the parties affected by such action would have the right to take the retaliatory action and can withdraw the equivalent concessions.

Rules of Origin

As per Article 16, the existing SAPTA rules of origin system is based upon import content norms. Presently, the total *c.i.f.* value of imported inputs is not allowed to exceed 50 per cent of the *f.o.b.* value of the products produced in a member country. In the case of inputs sourced from within the region, the regional content should not be more than 40 per cent of the products' *f.o.b.* value. The LDCs are given a special treatment in this regard. Products originating in these countries are allowed a favourable 10 per cent age points in the case of the above—mentioned percentages[7].

The existing rules of origin under the SAPTA regime are being viewed as one of the major factors responsible for impeding trade flows within the region. Many SAARC countries are of the opinion that the relaxed rules of origin under SAPTA would facilitate their exports to the region since their present stage of development does not allow them to undertake high value added activities. Lack of adequate natural and mineral resources along with limited domestic supply of intermediate and capital goods have made their economies quite dependent on imports, which prevent them to meet the local content requirement of the rules of origin under SAPTA.

Modification and Withdrawal of Concessions

The Agreement also has provisions regarding the modification and withdrawal of concessions if the Contracting State concerned finds that the anticipated results of the Agreement are not accruing to it, and the adverse impact of it are proportionately larger. It can do so after the lapse of three years from the day the concession was extended. As per Article 17, the procedure for it is as follows[8]:

- Any Contracting State may, after a period of three years from the day the concessions came into force, inform the Committee about its intention of modifying or withdrawing any concession included in its appropriate schedule.
- The Contracting State intending to withdraw or modify a concession would enter into consultation and negotiation with a view to reaching an agreement on any necessary and appropriate compensation with the Contracting State with which such concession was initially negotiated or any other State that has a substantial supplying interest.
- If no agreement is reached among the Contracting States concerned within 6 months of the receipt of notification and if the notifying State proceeds with its modification or withdrawal of such concessions, the affected Contracting States, as determined by the

Committee, may withdraw or modify equivalent concessions in their appropriate schedules. Any such modification or withdrawal must be notified to the Committee.

In this case, the Agreement gives opportunities to the affected Contracting States to negotiate the compensation for withdrawing or modifying the concession by any Contracting State. In case of failure to reach an agreement, there is also the provision of retaliation by the affected parties.

According to Article 18, a Contracting State would at any time be free to withhold or to withdraw in whole or in part any item in its schedule of concessions in respect of which it determines that it was initially negotiated with a state which has ceased to be a Contracting State in this Agreement. A Contracting State taking such action shall notify the Committee and, upon request, consult with other Contracting States that have a substantial interest in the product concerned.

Consultation is the soul of the whole SAPTA Agreement. As per Article 19, each Contracting State shall accord sympathetic consideration to and shall give adequate opportunities for consultations regarding such representations as may be made by another Contracting State with respect to any matter affecting the operation of this Agreement. The Committee may, at the request of a Contracting State, consult with any Contracting State in respect of any matter for which it has not been possible to find a satisfactory solution.

Withdrawal from SAPTA

There is also a provision for withdrawing the membership from the Agreement as per Article 21[9]. Such withdrawal would be effective after six months from the day a written notice thereof is received by the SAARC Secretariat, the depository of this Agreement. That Contracting State would simultaneously inform the Committee of the Action it has taken. The rights and obligations of a Contracting State, which has withdrawn from this Agreement, would cease to apply as of that effective date. Following the withdrawal by any Contracting State, the Committee shall meet within 30 days to consider action subsequent to withdrawal.

Notwithstanding the measures specified in Articles 4 and 6, the provisions of this Agreement would not apply in relation to preferences already granted or to be granted by any Contracting State to other Contacting States outside the framework of this Agreement, and to third countries through bilateral, plurilateral and multilateral trade agreements. The Contracting State would also not be obliged to grant preferences in SAPTA that impair the concessions extended under those agreements. It simply means that the concessions granted under the Trade and Transit Treaty by India to Nepal would not be affected with the conclusion of the SAPTA Agreement. Under this provision, India has also signed the Bilateral Free Trade Agreements with Bangladesh and Sri Lanka recently.

References

1. *National Schedule of Concessions: First and Second Round of SAPTA* (Ministry of Commerce & FICCI), p.3.
2. *Ibid.*,p.4
3. *Ibid.*, p. 5.
4. *Direction of Trade Statistics* (IMF), Yearbook, 1999.
5. Nationàl Schedule of concessions, N. 11, p.5.
6. *Ibid.*, pp.6-7
7. *Ibid.*, p.12-15.
8. *Ibid.*, P.7.
9. *Ibid.*, p. 9.

5

SAPTA—A Balance Sheet

The South Asian Region has been late to jump on the bandwagon of regional trading blocs (RTBs) as seen in previous chapters. Although the acceleration of economic growth through regional co-operation was incorporated as an objective in South Asian Association for Regional Co-operation (SAARC) Charter, it was not until 1987 Summit in Kathmandu that the SAARC leaders recognized the need for explicitly entering into South Asian Economic Co-operation (SAEC). The objective was to ensure more tangible benefits to the people of the region. It was argued that such benefits are to be generated through taking advantage of growing regional complementarities, their inter-dependence, and co-ordination of national policies and approaches for finding common solutions to their problems.

By the time of the 1988 Islamabad Summit, a group of experts had worked out the modalities for studies to be carried out for cooperation in the areas of trade, manufactures and services with the objective of meeting the basic needs of the people of the region. The Islamabad Summit directed the meeting of planners to examine the possibility of co-operation in these agreed areas, and to make specific recommendations. Following the recommendations of the SAARC Study on Trade, Manufactures and Services, the Committee for Economic Co-operation (CEC) was set up in 1991. The Colombo Summit in that year declared the leaders' commitment to the liberalisation of trade in the region through a step-by-step approach in such a manner that all the countries in the region share the benefits of trade expansion equitably.

The Inter-Government Group of Trade Experts (IGGTE) was set up to work out mutually acceptable trade liberalisation measures to examine Sri Lanka's proposal to establish a SAARC Preferential Trading Arrangement (SAPTA), and to formulate and seek agreement on an institutional framework for its implementation. Thus, eventually the SAPTA was finalised and signed in Dhaka in 1993. The first round of negotiations under SAPTA took place in 1995. By December 2000, three trade negotiations have been completed, under which 5553 items at Harmonised System (HS) six digit levels have been offered for tariff and non tariff concessions by the member states. India being the largest economy of the region, offered the maximum number of items (2925 items) for preferential trade.

From the second round onwards, the negotiations for removing the non-tariff barriers were also conducted. India has unilaterally withdrawn almost all non-tariff barriers in case of import from the members of SAPTA in 1998. The ranges of tariff concessions are 5 to 50 per cent in case of the relatively developed economies and 10 to 100 per cent in case of the least developed economies of the region. In most cases, however, the extent of tariff concession is 10 per cent of the basic tariff rates.

In the schedules of concessions submitted by the member states of SAPTA, concessions have been given in three ways. First, concessions exclusively applicable to the LDCs, second, concessions meant for both LDCs and non-LDCs (here the expressions like non- LDCs and other states also mean all member states), and third, concessions given against some items to both LDCs and non-LDCs. In the last case, LDCs would be eligible for the higher reduction in tariffs.

Like other regional trading blocs, SAARC also envisages the formation of a South Asian Free Trade Area (SAFTA) through dismantling all barriers to intra-regional trade by 2001. At present, India imports around 6,600 commodities at the maximum disaggregated level (8-digit) of Harmonised System (HS) from the world, of which only 324 originate from the SAARC countries. The conclusion of SAPTA (I) in 1995, SAPTA (II) in 1997 and SAPTA (III) in 1998 are the preliminary steps towards the objective of achieving totally free trade under SAFTA.

SAPTA (I)

The first round of trade negotiations under SAPTA was given final shape in the seventh summit held in April 1993. Under this round, each SAARC country offered preferential tariffs to other member countries of SAARC by reducing tariffs on specific commodities / commodity groups. Ultimately, SAPTA (I) came into force in December 1995 after being notified by all the constituent members of SAARC. In SAPTA (I), the tariff concessions were offered on 226 commodities by all member countries, of which 100 were offered to the least developed countries (LDCs) only.[1] Among all the SAARC nations, India submitted a schedule of the maximum commodities (106 items), offering concessions ranging from 10-100 per cent. Out of 106 items, India offered 62 items to LDCs only.

Bangladesh made an offer for 12 items, Bhutan presented a list offering concessions for 14 items, and Maldives' list comprised 17 items. Nepal presented a small list of 11 items. Pakistan's list was of 35 items and Sri Lanka presented a schedule for 31 items.

Under SAPTA (I), every member country presented a list of offer for tariff concessions, identifying the commodities as per their choice. However, once the concessions were offered, they were applicable to all the member countries save in cases exclusively meant for the least developed countries.

Table 5.1 shows the break up of the tariff lines offered for concession by all member states. In the total of 106 items offered by India for the preferential access, 62 items were meant for the LDCs only and 64 items for the non-LDCs. Bangladesh offered 1 item to the LDCs and 11 items to the non-LDCs in a total of 12 items, Sri Lanka made available 20 and 11 items for the non-LDCs and the LDCs respectively in a total of 31 items and Pakistan's concessional schedule consisted of 20 items for non-

LDCs and 15 items for LDCs making a total of 35 items. Nepal offered 10 items for non-LDCs and 4 items for LDCs in a total of 14 items, Bhutan presented a list of concessions comprising 7 items for LDCs and 4 items for other countries in a total of 11 items and of the LDCs, Maldives offered the maximum total items (17), all for all member countries.

TABLE 5.1

SAPTA (I)—Consolidated National Schedule of Concessions Number of Tariff Lines Agreed (HS-6 DIGIT)

Country	Total Commodities Offered for Concession	Commodities for Non-LDCs	Commoditie s for LDCs
India	106	44	62
Bangladesh	12	11	01
Sri Lanka	31	20	11
Pakistan	35	20	15
Nepal	14	10	04
Bhutan	11	04	07
Maldives	17	17	00
Total	**226**	**126**	**100**

Source: National Schedule of Concessions : First and Second Round of SAPTA (Ministry of Commerce and FICCI).

Analysing the impact of SAPTA (I) on the overall trade creation within the bloc, it was negligible for the following reasons:

- The trade is not restricted by tariffs only but the existence of non-tariff and other barriers are equally important.
- The commodity coverage under SAPTA (I) by each member country was too low to make any perceptible impact on the overall trade creation among SAARC nations.
- The weight of these commodities in total trade was almost negligible compared to the total import baskets of these respective countries. The fact shows that out of the 106 commodities offered for concession under

SAPTA (I) by India, it hardly imported 23 items from the SAARC countries in 1993-94. Bangladesh offered preferential access for 12 items, of which it imported only six items from India in 1992-93. On the other hand, Pakistan has so far not extended MFN status to India under WTO. It has only identified almost 600 items eligible for import from India, out of which it offered preferential access to only 35 products. However, it imported only 13 products from India in 1993-94. Nepal offered concessions for 11 items under SAPTA (I), of which it imported only three items from India during 1993-94. The total items offered for concession by Sri Lanka were 31, but it barely imported 17 products from Indian in 1993-94. As far as the coverage ratio is concerned, Sri Lanka fares well among all the SAARC members.

- Moreover, the extent of tariff concession was also not substantial. Although it ranged from 10 to 100 per cent, on most of the commodities it was just 10 per cent of the basic duty.

As a result of all these factors, the trade increase among SAARC nations due to the implementation of SAPTA (I) was negligible. It increased from $1435 million in 1993-94 to $1937 million in 1997-98. This increase in trade is more in value terms owing to increase in prices and less in volume terms. As a percentage of total exports of the region to the world, it was of the same level–3.8 per cent in 1993-94 and 1997-98.[2]

SAPTA (II)

The consolidated national schedules submitted under SAPTA (II) in March 1997 have more extensive coverage of goods than under SAPTA (I). In terms of coverage of the products, SAPTA (II) covers a total of 1871 items at 6-digit level, as shown in Table 5.2. India's offer covers the largest number of items, giving tariff concessions for 902 items. Out of these,

512 items were meant for tariff concessions to LDCs only and the rest, 390 items, were offered to all the countries including LDCs and non-LDCs. The range of duty concessions offered by India varies from 10 per cent to 50 per cent, depending on the commodity and the country concerned. Obviously, the rate of tariff concession offered to LDCs is relatively higher compared to non-LDCs. There are two rates of reduction of duties in case of LDCs–25 per cent and 50 per cent. For non-LDCs, these concessions are 10 per cent, 15 per cent, 25 per cent and 40 per cent. Even in the items made available for concession for both LDCs and non-LDCs, the LDCs were given better preferential access than non-LDCs by granting them higher reduction in tariff rates. It is evident from the consolidated schedules that for some items, two rates of concession in tariffs have been given–one applicable to LDCs and second to all member countries. In such cases, a higher reduction of duties to LDCs will hold good.

Pakistan's schedule for concessions covers 363 items in all, out of which, 131 items are granted for concession to only LDCs and rest are open to all countries. Like India it has also given more market access to LDCs than non-LDCs by offering more tariff reduction to LDCs as compared to other countries. It offered tariff concession of 15 per cent in case of LDCs and 10 per cent in case of all member states. Sri Lanka offers 95 items in total for tariff concessions, out of which 23 items to LDCs only and the remaining 72 items to all member states. The rates of reduction offered by it to LDCs are 10 per cent, 50 per cent and 60 per cent, whereas it has offered a flat rate of 10 per cent for tariff reduction for all commodities to non-LDCs.

In the second round of negotiations, Bangladesh presented a list of 226 items for tariff concession; 11 items were offered to the least developed countries only, while all member states were given the remaining 215 items. The rate of concession is a flat rate of 10 per cent for countries of both categories. Bhutan submitted a list offering concessions for 47 commodities in total, of which 10 items for LDCs only and the rest for non-LDCs. It gave 15 per cent duty reduction to LDCs and 10 per cent to all countries. Nepal has presented a relatively larger list in comparison to other least developed countries of the region, including 233 commodities for preferential access. It includes 67 items for LDCs only and the rest 166 for all the member states. To LDCs, it has offered concessions of 15 per cent and 10 per cent, whereas to non-LDCs, it has offered a 10 per cent reduction. Maldives presented the smallest list for concessions comprising only five items. It provided 3 items for LDCs and 2 items for non-LDCs, giving them 15 per cent and 10 per cent concessions respectively. The number of items offered for concession by different SAARC countries and the extent of reduction in basic duties have been show in Table 5.2.

TABLE 5.2

SAPTA (II)—Consolidated National Schedules of Concessions Number of Tariff Lines Agreed (HS-6 Digit)

Country	For all Countries	Only for LDCs	Total
Bangladesh	215 (10%)	11 (10%)	226
Bhutan	37 (10%)	10 (15%)	47
India	390 (10%, 15%, 25% and 40%)	512 (25%, 50%)	902
Maldives	2 (10%)	3 (15%)	5
Nepal	166 (10%)	67 (15% and 10%)	233
Pakistan	232 (10%)	131 (15%)	363
Sri Lanka	72 (10%)	23 (10%, 50% and 60%)	95
Total	**1114**	**757**	**1871**

Source: SAARC Secretariat, SAPTA: A status note as on March 1997, Economic Division, SAARC Secretariat, Katmandu.

Another important feature of the second round of negotiations is that it has listed all important Non-Tariff Barriers (NTBs) with particular reference to QRs (Quantitative Restrictions). For example, the schedule of proposed concessions granted by India to Bangladesh contains NTBs like importables against license, special import license (SIL), importables against SIL and restricted items. These NTBs have been relaxed in case of LDCs. The NTBs to India's import from Pakistan include importables against license, canalized imports and permitted against SIL. While examining the gravity of trade restrictions in terms of NTBs, it is clear from the sehedule that out of the 902 items offered for concession by India to both LDCs and non-LDCs, 195 items are subject to NTBs, of which 177 items are imported from LDCs and 18 items from non-LDCs. The list of NTBs in Pakistan schedule is much more extensive, which are basically QRs. The other member states have not given the NTBs against items included in concession schedules except in case of a few items.

As a result of the implementation of SAPTA (II), the increase in trade among the SAARC nations has been relatively satisfactory. It increased from $ 1937 million in 1997-98 to $ 2567 million in 1998-99. As a percentage of total exports of the region to the world, it increased to 4.8 per cent in 1998-99 from 3.8 per cent in 1997-98.[3]

SAPTA (III)

The third meeting of the Inter-Governmental Group on Trade Liberalisation to conclude the third round of trade negotiations under SAPTA was held at the SAARC Secretariat, Kathmandu on 21-23 November 1998. The meeting, attended by the representatives of all SAARC member countries, was opened by Naeen U. Hasan, Secretary General, SAARC Secretariat, Kathmandu.

After intensive deliberations, the delegates exchanged national schedules of concessions under SAPTA (III). It was agreed that the consolidated schedules should be sent to the Secretariat not later than December 20, 1998. Under SAPTA (III), another 3456 commodities at HS-6 digit level were included under preferential regime.[4] India again offered the maximum number of items (1917 items) for preferential access along with deepening the tariff concessions on commodities already included under the SAPTA (I) and SAPTA (II) negotiations. On all tariff lines, agreed to in the First and Second Rounds, where the preference was 25 per cent or below, it has been enhanced to 50 per cent, and tariff lines where the preference granted was above 25 per cent and up to 50 per cent, it has been enhanced to 60 per cent.[5] Maldives, Bangladesh and Pakistan presented the lists including 368 items, 481 items and 295 items respectively. Bhutan, Nepal and Sri Lanka gave concession on 124, 189 and 82 tariff lines respectively.

India gave tariff concessions of 50 per cent for LDCs and 10 per cent, 20 per cent and 25 per cent for non-LDCs. Nepal gave tariff concessions of 10 and 15 per cent to LDCs and 10 per cent to non-LDCs. Bangladesh and Pakistan provided reduction of 10 and 15 per cent, and 30 per cent for LDCs and 10 per cent and 20 per cent for non-LDCs respectively. Bhutan's concessions were 10 and 20 per cent for LDCs and 10 per cent for non-LDCs.

Under SAPTA (III), an attempt has been made to further relax the Non-Tariff Barriers (NTBs). India withdrew all non-tariffs barriers (NTBs) regarding quantitative restrictions vis-a-vis all SAPTA member countries in 1998. However, Pakistan has still not granted India the MFN status under WTO.

Analysing the impact of SAPTA (III) on the overall trade creation within the SAARC region, it may be noted that the trade has increased to $2046 million in the first three quarters of 1999-2000 from $1925 million during the same duration in 1998-99. It increased from 4.8 per cent to 4.9 per cent of the total region's exports to the world during the same periods.[6]

During the third round of negotiations, the representatives of member states of SAPTA decided to initiate the fourth round of negotiations at the earliest, possibly in March 1999. It was decided that during the fourth round, an endeavour would be made to conduct trade negotiations preferably chapter-wise, on sectoral basis or across-the-board in order to make more substantive progress on trade negotiations within the region, keeping in mind special interests and concerns of the LDCs. It was further decided to expand the products' coverage substantially so that from the fourth round onwards, the process of launching South Asian Free Trade Area (SAFTA) may be accelerated.

It was also decided that in the fourth round of negotiations, a serious consideration would be given to further deepening of concessions already given in the first three rounds. The representatives of the member states also felt the need to devise a formula so as to bring some equity in margins of preference to be granted by the Contracting States. Recalling the decision taken at the Colombo Summit, the representatives also stressed the urgency in finalising the SAFTA Treaty, for which a Committee of Experts was to be constituted. The Sri Lankan delegation informed the meeting that they already had drafted the Terms of Reference for this Committee.

The member states agreed to provide copies of their latest tariff and trade-related documents and published as well as computerised data bases on a regular basis to the SAARC Secretariat to strengthen the data base available in the Secretarial. It would also enable the Secretariat to maintain and update trade control measures of the SAARC member countries. They also felt the need to harmonise the national regimes of intellectual property rights. In this context, the Meeting noted that the World Intellectual Property Organization (WIPO) was organising a sub-regional forum on Intellectual Property Cooperation among the SAARC countries in cooperation with the Government of Sri Lanka. They also decided to examine carefully the liberalisation of trade in services within SAPTA during the fourth round of negotiations.

However, the fourth round of negotiations has not been launched so far. It has delayed the whole process of converting SAPTA into SAFTA by 2001 as envisaged in the original plan. The reason for this delay on purely economic ground is the fear of relatively small states of the region that the maximum benefits of opening up within the region would accrue to relatively larger economies of the region, especially India. They have the feeling that their economies would be swamped by Indian goods. Among other reasons, which are more political in nature, there is the prolonged tangle between India and Pakistan over Kashmir. The recent Kargil episode has pushed all efforts of realising SAFTA backward by at least 4 to 5 years. In other worlds, now the realisation of SAFTA would be delayed by at least 4 to 5 years because of further erosion of goodwill between India and Pakistan, two important members of the bloc. The end of the democratic governance and take over by the military regime in Pakistan are other blows against achieving the goal of SAFTA.

Status of SAPTA

For SAPTA's conversion into SAFTA, all tariff and non-tariff barriers are required to be dismantled so as to allow the free movement of goods within the bloc. By this criterion, SAPTA is yet to go a long way because, as of 2000, after the conclusion of three rounds of negotiations, only a total 5553 tariff lines at H S-6 digit levels have been brought under preferential regime if concessions given by all member states are taken into consideration as a whole. India has offered the maximum number of items by including the 2925 tariff lines under the preferential system. However, India at 6-digit level imports 5063 items. This gives an idea of the large number of tariff lines which are to be brought under the preferential regime by all member states as a first necessary step towards realisation of SAFTA. Moreover, the extent of tariff concession has to be made 100 per cent on all tariff lines. Till now, although the extent of tariff concession in case of LDCs and non-LDCs varies from 10 to 100 per cent and 5 to 50 per cent respectively, on most of the items, it is below 20 per cent. Further, the non-tariff barriers (NTBs), which are very prominent in the region as a policy matter owing to perennially unfavourable balance of payment positions of these countries and their pursuing the inward looking import- substitution policies, have also to be withdrawn within the region. Though, from the second round of negotiations onwards, NTBs have also been included for negotiations, and they have been relaxed in case of LDCs, it is still a long way to go in this regard. Negotiating non-tariff barriers within the region would be a more difficult task. However, India has unilaterally withdrawn all its NTBs regarding quantitative restrictions in case of imports from within the SAPTA region in 1998.

These non-tariff barriers are also inconsistent with the WTO provisions, albeit the developing countries can maintain them on the pretext of their precarious balance of payment (BOP) positions. However, after India losing its case in Dispute Settlement Body (DSB) of WTO and Indo-US agreement, it will have to dismantle all its quantitative restrictions (QRs) by April 2001. Before April 2000, India was maintaining QRs on 1426 tariff lines. Half of these tariff lines were freed in the Exim Policy Modifications (2000-2001), and the remaining half liberalised this year. These QRs will now be replaced by tariff equivalents. But other countries of the region can still maintain them because of their unfavourable BOP positions under WTO. Negotiating them among member states of the SAPTA bloc would be an uphill task.

It can thus be safely concluded that the South Asian region is not even half way through in terms of achieving the goal of SAFTA. It has yet to traverse a long way to achieve this goal. A study conducted by Associated Chambers of Commerce and Industry of India (ASSOCHAM) roughly estimated that out of the total items (5553) brought under preferential regime under SAPTA, the trade-intensive items (in which trade is of substantial level) are not more than 150 items. In fact, the member states have adopted a faulty approach by including mostly non-trade-intensive commodities in schedules of concessions.

As mandated by the Ninth SAARC Summit (1997), a Group of Eminent Persons (GEP) was constituted to further study, *inter alia*, ways and means of enhancing the effectiveness of SAARC in achieving its objectives especially in the economic field. It submitted its report in 1999, charting out a roadmap for converting the SAPTA into SAFTA, then into South Asian Customs Union (SACU) and finally into South Asian Economic Union (SAEU) by the year 2020.[7]

GEP's main recommendation is to establish a South Asian Economic Union (SAEU) by the year 2020 in successive stages. In the first stage, South Asian Free Trade Area (SAFTA) should be created. The transition from SAPTA to SAFTA should be through negotiations and implementation of a comprehensive inter-governmental treaty in conformity with article XXIV of the WTO. As per the GEP report, negotiations for it should start in 1999 and the implementation should be initiated in the beginning of the year 2000 to be completed by 2010 in the case of least developed member states, and by 2008 in case of other member states.

In the second stage, a South Asian Custom Union (SACU) should be created preferably by the year 2015. The third stage should see the coming into being of the South Asian Economic Union (SAEU) by the year 2020. The process for this should be initiated 4 to 5 years in advance.

According to the report, all non-tariff barriers, including discriminatory practices, should be identified during the first year of the implementation period and should be phased out over the next 9 years by the least developed countries, and over 7 years by other countries. A possible method of eliminating tariffs on all trade could be a 12.5 per cent reduction per annum over the 8 years period. However, alternative approaches and sequencing for achieving the same goal can be explored by drawing upon the experiences of other regional groupings in establishing free trade areas.

The GEP took special care of LDCs and recommended that it must be ensured right from the beginning that the least developed member states are able to take full advantage of freeing the trade by other member states and, in general, to benefit equitably from the integration process. For this purpose, it recommended the following special measures for LDCs:[8]

- A longer time-period for freeing trade
- Staggering the process of freeing trade in particular sectors
- Resort to safeguard measures for a longer period
- Creation of a special fund for compensating the loss of revenue suffered as a result of reducing or eliminating tariffs by the LDCs.
- Creation of a reasonably large sized fund for the development of their infrastructure, human resources and export production and diversification capacity.
- Facilitating free movement of private capital to the least developed countries from the member countries.
- Special relaxation in rules of origin to LDCs.

The GEP has laid down the roadmap for creating the South Asian Economic Union by the year 2020. However, realising the delays already made and progress achieved so far in terms of opening up economies by the member states, it deviates from the original plan of achieving SAFTA by 2001. It has earmarked sufficient time for it now—2010 for LDCs and 2008 for non-LDCs. It goes beyond the Articles 6 and 10 of the SAPTA Agreement while recommending special care for LDCs.

Will Regional Bloc be Successful in South Asia?

The success of SAFTA ultimately hinges on its generating a substantial amount of trade within the region. As is evident from Section I, the regional trading blocs are more successful in developed countries in comparison to developing ones. As was stated earlier, the developed countries have well developed industrial structures based on sophisticated technologies, which allow them to develop and specialize in the differential products of the same items enhancing complementarities among them. The developing countries, on the contrary, are basically dominated by agriculture sector with weak industrial structures limiting the scope for complementarities among them. The South Asian region also comprises the developing and least developed economies. Out of seven countries of the region, four are the least developed countries. In such a scenario, will creating regional trading bloc be a success in South Asia?

The economies of the South Asian region have mainly the agriculture sector contributing a major part to their GDPs, albeit the share of agriculture to G.D.P. has come down of late in South Asia. It was around 40 per cent in 1980, which has come down to 25 per cent in 1997. Still it is the main occupation here employing more than 50 per cent of the work force of the region. The industrial sector, though growing, is still at the nascent stage in South Asia with varying levels of development. India and Sri Lanka have comparatively developed industrial structures contributing almost 30% to their GDPs.

Before analysing the potential of trade creation among the SAARC nations after establishing the full-fledged SAFTA, it would be worthwhile to look at the present status of intra-regional trade within the SAARC region and compare it with other regional trading blocs of the world.

As is evident from Tables 5.3 and 5.4, the trade among SAPTA member countries has increased from 3.2 per cent in 1990 to 4.3 per cent of total exports of SAARC region to the world in 1996. It further increased to 4.8 per cent in the year 1998-99.Though the trade among the SAARC member states has gone up after the formation of SAPTA, it is much lower in comparison to the growth of trade within EU, NAFTA and ASEAN. In NAFTA, the intra-regional trade was to the tune of 33.6% of the total region's exports to the world in 1980. It increased to 41.4 per cent in 1990 and 47.5 per cent in 1996. In the case of EU and ASEAN, the intra-regional trade figures were 61 per cent in 1980, 66 per cent in 1990 and 61.5 per cent in 1996 of the total region's exports to the world for EU, and 16.9 per cent, 18.7 per cent and 23.2 per cent for the same periods respectively for ASEAN. Even the MERCOSUR, which is the regional trading group of South American developing countries including Argentina, Brazil, Paraguay and Uruguay, have much more impressive intra-regional trade performance than that of SAPTA. It was 8.9 per cent in 1990, rising to 28.8 per cent of region's total exports to world in 1996. Thus, the intra-regional trade is much lower within the SAARC region in comparison to other regional blocs of the world. It reflects the lack of complementarities among the SAARC nations.

TABLE 5.3

Exports within Regional Economic Groupings

(% of Total Exports)

Regions	1980	1990	1996
NAFTA	33.6	41.4	47.5
EU	61.0	66.0	61.5
MERCOSUR	11.6	8.9	22.8
ASEAN	16.9	18.7	23.2
SAARC	4.8	3.2	4.3

Source: World Bank : World Development Indicators, 1998.

In South Asia, the industrial sector as a whole is employing low level of technologies. It is mainly dominated by agro-based and labour-intensive industries, like textile, sugar, leather products, etc. As mentioned earlier, in these types of industries, there is very little scope for having product differentiation, and for that reason, there is less chance for complementarities. However, India, Sri Lanka and Pakistan have comparatively advanced industries. India is doing extremely well in information technology-based industries, becoming a global player in this area.

TABLE-5.4

Intra-Regional Exports among SAARC Members Countries

(Percentage of Total World)

Origin / Destination	Year	Bangladesh	India	Nepal	Pakistan	Sri Lanka	Total SAARC
Bangladesh	1995	—	0.64	0.3	1.04	0.06	1.85
India	1996	2.57	—	0.49	0.45	1.42	4.92
Nepal	1996	1.45	9.54	—	—	—	10.98
Pakistan	1996	1.17	0.44	0.06	—	0.86	2.54
Sri Lanka	1996	0.29	1.05	0.02	0.90	—	2.27

Source: IMF, Direction of Trade Statistics Year Book, 1997 and Quarterly March, 1998.

In agriculture sector also, the South Asian countries have more or less similar patterns of production because they lie almost within the same band of latitudinal positions, albeit there are some climatic variations owing to different terrain. For example, Bhutan and Nepal have mainly mountainous terrain, whereas Maldives and Sri Lanka are islands and have large coastal areas. These variations in terrain and resultantly in climatic conditions give some scope of complementarities among countries of the region. For instance Sri Lanka and Maldives are good in marine products.

Thus, it is clear from the above analysis that the economies of the South Asian region have almost similar patterns of production with little variation leading to lack of complementarities among them. For instance, at present India imports around 6600 commodities or commodity groups at the maximum disaggregated level (8-digit) of the harmonised system from the world, of which only 324 originate from SAARC countries.

Measures to Increase Complementarities Among States of South Asia

Exploring the ways and means of increasing complementarities, indispensable for making a bloc meaningful on the economic grounds, among the member states of the SAARC, one can categorize them into two groups. One is the automatic mechanism, in-built in the opening- up process, and second is through intervention by the respective governments of the member states of the region.

Let us take the first category of the automatic in-built mechanism. The basic principle of international trade is that when the process of opening up starts through step-by-step dismantling of the tariff and non-tariff barriers, countries start switching over to the patterns of production where they have the maximum comparative advantages. This is a universal principle, which is equally applicable to all sectors of economy including agriculture, industry as well as service sectors. It is obvious that after the total elimination of tariff and non-tariff barriers, a country cannot face competition from outside in those items where it does not have comparative advantages. Earlier, in the protective environment, these items were artificially made economically viable through restricting competition from outside by tariff and non-tariff barriers. Thus, it is the in-built mechanism of liberalisation of international trade that ensures the complementarities. The same principle works in an economic integration scheme in a region under a regional trading bloc. When a regional trading bloc moves on to the second stage of evolution of a bloc from Preferential Trading Arrangement to Free Trade Area and then Custom Union, it is required to withdraw in phases all tariff and non-tariff barriers. In the process, it would compel the entrepreneurs of the region to switch over to those items where their respective countries have comparative advantages.

Hence, it is also expected to happen in case of the economic integration scheme currently underway in South Asia. However, in the South Asian region, there are 4 least developed countries out of the total 7 constituting the region. These LDCs have production baskets with limited items comprising mainly agricultural or primary goods. The opening up process in the region would certainly increase trade with these economies, but it would be mainly one-way increase due to production baskets of these LDCs having limited items. Moreover, even this increase in trade would be limited owing to the lack of purchasing power in these states. Such position will never be to the liking of LDCs as it will increase their trade deficit with the relatively developed economies of the region. Moreover, they will always have a feeling of fear that their economies would be flooded with goods originating from the larger economies of the region even in those areas where they have relatively natural advantages. To allay these fears, measures involving governmental interventions, discussed at the later part of this sub-section, would be of great help.

In order to analyse the potential of trade creation among the relatively bigger economies of the region, a careful look at the patterns of production of these economies is necessary. They have more or less similar production baskets comprising some items with large comparative advantages for some country, some items with a small comparative advantages for another country and some common items with same comparative advantages for every country. Commodities with large comparative advantages include, for example, plantation crops and marine products for Sri Lanka and industrial products, like engineering products and IT products, for India. Bangladesh has absolute advantage in jute processing, while Pakistan has large comparative advantages with in sugar, fruits, nuts and spices, etc. The volume of trade is bound to grow in these items with the trade liberalisation under the regional economic integration scheme. The commodity groups with less or same comparative advantages include food products, textiles, paper products, non-metallic and mineral products, etc.

As was stated earlier also, the complementarities among economies would increase as the economies of the region move on to more developed industrial structures based on sophisticated technologies. The industrial structures of SAARC countries have moved towards diversification in a sustained manner over the past decade. Table 5.5 presents the specialisation indices for SAPTA Member Countries (SMCs) for the 1985-95 period.[9] The specialisation index indicates the extent of specialisation of the manufacturing industry in a country. It is equal to 100 if the country specialises in only one industry and would be equal to zero if the shares of all branches of industry are equal. Thus higher the value of the specialisation index, lower would be the extent of diversification of industrial structure of a country and vice-versa.

It is apparent from the Table 5.5 that though the degree of specialisation has declined over 1985-95 period for all the SAARC countries, the extent of change varies across the countries. Most impressive movement towards diversification of the industrial structure has been recorded by Sri Lanka from an index of 30 to 20, closely followed by Nepal from 26.1 to 17.5. India has recorded a 23.3 per cent decline in the levels of specialisation, and it is 17.5 per cent in the case of Pakistan. The progress towards diversification in the case of Bangladesh has been rather slow with only a 2 per cent increase over a decade. Another feature that is evident from the Table is that India has the most diversified, and Bangladesh, the least manufacturing industry in the SAARC region.

TABLE 5.5

Degree of Specialisation of Manufacturing Sector in SAPTA Member Countries (SMCs)

Country	1985	1990	1995
Bangladesh	25.3	24.9	24.8
Bhutan	N.A.	N.A.	N.A.
India	16.9	15.3	13.7
Maldives	N.A.	N.A.	N.A.
Nepal	26.1	20.5	17.5
Pakistan	23.5	23.4	20.0
Sri Lanka	30.0	23.5	20.0

Source: *Compiled from UNIDO, Industry and Development: Global Report, 1997* by RIS in SAARC Survey of Development and Cooperation 1998/99.

Note: Based on Shares of 29 branches (at 3-digit level) of manufacturing industry with manufacturing value added.

The changing composition of manufacturing value added over the past decade of SMCs across 9 broad sectors has been given in Table 5.6. It is clear that food products and textiles and apparel industries account for a large chunk of manufacturing value added in SMCs except for India. The relatively more modern industries *viz.* engineering (covering electrical and non–electrical machinery and equipment and automotive industries),

TABLE 5.6

Composition of Manufacturing Value added in SMCs

Sector	Bangladesh		Nepal		India		Pakistan		Sri Lanka	
	1985	**1995**	**1985**	**1995**	**1985**	**1995**	**1985**	**1995**	**1985**	**1995**
Food Produces	24.7	25.4	50.0	34.6	11.6	11.9	31.7	23.6	62.6	43.6
Textiles and Apparel	30.3	36.6	19.0	33.9	16.0	15.4	19.1	22.5	15.2	20.3
Wood Products	1.4	1.0	3.0	2.8	0.5	1.0	0.5	1.0	1.8	1.0
Paper Products	3.1	4.4	3.0	2.6	3.3	3.7	2.1	3.5	3.1	3.3
Chemical and Allie Products	27.2	17.4	6.0	7.8	21.7	27.3	19.6	22.4	6.1	6.5
Non-Metallic Mineral Products	1.7	2.8	12.0	8.3	5.8	4.1	6.9	9.3	6.1	5.2
Metals	4.1	4.0	2.0	2.1	12.3	10.9	10.6	6.5	1.0	1.5
Engineering Products	6.7	8.1	4.0	7.3	28.9	24.9	9.3	11.4	3.4	6.1
Other Manufactures	1.0	1.0	1.0	0.5	1.0	1.0	1.0	1.0	1.0	2.6
Total	**100**	**100**	**100**	**100**	**100**	**100**	**100**	**100**	**100**	**100**

Source: RIS figures based on data presented in UNIDO, *Industry and Development: Global Report*, 1997.

chemical and allied product industries account for relatively minor shares in the manufacturing value added in most SMCs except for India. In case of India, these industries accounted for over half of the manufacturing value added. However, all the SAARC countries except India have seen rising importance of engineering industries as a contributor to manufacturing value added. Nepal has recorded the most impressive increase in the importance of engineering industries with an 82 per cent rise in its share over the decade, followed by Sri Lanka with 74 per cent. Pakistan and Bangladesh have recorded 22 and 21 per cent increase respectively. The other perceptible fact is the increasing importance of textiles and apparel industry in manufacturing value added in all SMCs that has emerged as one of the most important sectors for export oriented manufacture in the region.[10]

As far as increasing complimentarities through the second method, intervention by respective governments, is concerned, some ways and means have already been spelt out in the GEP report mentioned earlier and articles 6 and 10 of the SAPTA Agreement to increase complementarities by increasing the export capacities of the LDCs. There is a need to look beyond these measures. Some initiatives should come from the private entrepreneurs of the comparatively better off economies. They should explore the possibilities of establishing joint ventures not only in LDCs but also in other countries as well for mutual benefits. These joint ventures should be tied with the buy-back arrangement. It will certainly be beneficial for both the parties participating in the joint venture and will create trade for both the countries. It would also sharpen the competitive edge of the countries because of the economies of scale and combination of best factors of production of the region, which in turn, would also help in international market outside the bloc. The joint ventures can be established at a more favourable location as per the nature of industries, which might help them reduce the cost of production.

A suggestion, in this regard, may be made for India to establish Special Economic Zones (SEZs), based on the Chinese model, at the borders with Bangladesh, Pakistan, Nepal and Bhutan. Some fiscal and monetary incentives should be announced by the respective governments—Indian as well as partner country's—to motivate the private entrepreneurs to move into these Special Economic Zones. This move should help motivate the private enterprises. In those countries, for example, Nepal and Bhutan, where there are not much private sector participation in the economic activities, the government can participate in such joint ventures. Some economists have expressed doubts about the effectiveness of the proposed measure in attracting the private sector. The author, however, is of the view that if incentives given are substantial enough to outweigh the negative factors and with flexible labour policy, facility of 100 per cent retention of the foreign exchange proceeds, etc., the private entrepreneurs would certainly move into these Special Economic Zones (SEZs). Establishing a world class infrastructure would be an added incentive. The joint ventures in these Special Economic Zones may be established in consumer products (edible oils, vanaspati, milk products and milk, textile products both synthetic and cotton base, sugar, etc.), consumer durables (TV both color and black and white, stainless steel utensils, cooking gadgets, watches, fans, low cost air conditioners/ air coolers, etc.) drugs and pharmaceuticals (basic drugs formulations, traditional medicines) and infrastructure development (Power generation and distribution, road construction, telecom services, port development ,etc).

The complementarities can also be increased through inviting foreign direct investment from outside the bloc in areas involving advanced technologies, like engineering products, automobiles, etc. The process is already on with each member country having realised the importance of FDI as a source of economic development and pursuing the policy of openness in this regard.

The border trade, which is not included in the SAPTA Agreement, can also be introduced. It will help the local small producers of the villages on both sides of the border, as they would be able to experience the economies of scale. Moreover, It would also be beneficial to the local populace of border villages, as they would be able to meet out their daily needs within a small radius without worrying about the border between two countries. Furthermore, the proposed measure would also formalise and regulate the illegal trade on the borders, which remains unnoticed because of the absence of such mechanism. Some points on the borders can be established for such border trade. It would help increase the overall trade turnover in the region.

References

1. *SAARC-Survey of Development and co-operation1998/99* [Research and Information System (RIS) for the Non- Aligned & Other Developing Countries] p.135.
2. *Direction of Trade Statistics*(IMF) -Year Book,1998
3. *Ibid.*
4. *Report of the Third Meeting of the Inter- Governmental Group on Trade Liberalization to Conclude the Third Round of Trade Negotiations under SAPTA* (SAARC Secretariat, Katmandu).
5. ''National Schedules of Concessions Granted by India'' http://www.saarcnet.org
6. *Direction of Trade Statistics* (Quarterly), March 2000,IMF
7. *Executive Summery and Recommendations of the Report of the Group of Eminent Persons (GEP)*, p.vi
8. *Ibid.*, pp.vi, vii.
9. *SAARC–Survey of Development and Cooperation1998/99* (RIS), p. 29.
10. *Ibid.*, p 30.

6

Conclusion

The failure of Indo-Pak Agra Summit held in July, 2001 is not only a setback to the widely desired improvement in the relations between the two countries but also to the much-needed progress in the multi- dimensional cooperation, especially economic, under the SAARC. The work under SAPTA-SAARC Preferential Trading Arrangement has ground to a halt after the third round of negotiations in 1998. It seems to have become a hostage of deteriorating relations between India and Pakistan largely on account of their territorial dispute over Kashmir. This is at a time when there is renewed emphasis on strengthening of economic ties under regional arrangements all the world over in the wake of collapse of the Seattle Ministerial Meet of WTO. It is unfortunate for the South Asian region that the countries of the region still attach high importance to the trivial zero-sum territorial disputes at the expense of non-zero-sum economic cooperation. This is in opposition to the time-tested fact of economic cooperation leading to sinking of political differences. Regional cooperation is all the more important in South Asia, as the region is inhabited by a large number of poor and illiterate people. Notwithstanding all pervasive poverty and deprivation, the decisions of the countries of the region seem to be dominated by political considerations, which, more often than not, defy economic sense.

It is surprising to note that even after the lapse of more than five years of the WTO coming into existence, Pakistan has not extended the Most Favoured Nation (MFN) status to India. Pakistan still allows just 615 items to be imported from India. To improve the economic ties between the two countries, an institutional arrangement at the level of industry associations of the two countries was forged in 1999. Federation of Indian Chamber of Commerce and Industry (FICCI) and Federation of Pakistan Chamber of Commerce and Industry (FPCCI) came together to set up India-Pakistan Chamber of Commerce and Industry (I-PCCI). Though the bilateral trade between the two countries has shown increasing trend in the 1990s, it has been much below its potential.

Not that the leaders of the region do not recognise the importance of all-round cooperation, especially economic. They have made umpteen attempts in this direction, but they got either derailed or blocked because of the dominance of bilateral issues over the common good. One such attempt was made in 1985 by forging the South Asian Association for Regional Cooperation (SAARC), and thereafter conducting the first round of trade negotiations under the SAARC Preferential Trading Arrangement (SAPTA) in 1995

The regional trading blocs (RTBs) are allowed under WTO, the successor of GATT, as per article XXIV. The article XXIV has two conditions for establishing a bloc. The first is that the trade restrictions among countries forming the bloc must be eliminated over a period, normally not exceeding 10 years. They can not be reimposed later. The second condition is that the common external tariffs levied after forming the bloc must not be higher than the average level of tariffs that existed in the member countries before the bloc was formed. These conditions, which are very loose, are being exploited by the developed countries to strengthen their regional economic blocs at the expense of non-bloc countries. Under these circumstances, it has become all the more necessary for the developing South Asian countries to take urgent steps to upgrade their regional economic cooperation under the SAARC.

Most of the countries are opening up their economies at two levels–one, at multilateral level under WTO, and second, at the regional level under regional arrangements. The opening up is faster and deeper at the regional level to give preferential treatment to the member countries of the group. Some economists are of the view that such regional groupings are against the Most Favoured Clause (MFN)- clause, the soul of the whole philosophy of WTO. However, the aim of allowing them under WTO is to expedite the process of dismantling the trade-distorting barriers–tariff and non-tariff, which is the ultimate goal of WTO.

The countries belonging to strong regional trading blocs having substantial intra-bloc trade, like NAFTA, EU, etc., are at an advantage at the cost of countries included in weak blocs or countries outside regional arrangements. The reason is that the members of a strong regional bloc are able to cut their imports from outside the bloc owing to the massive trade creation within the bloc resulting from preferential access accorded to them under the regional arrangement. This arrangement leads to marginalisation of the non-member countries. The countries in a weak bloc will not be able to create much trade within the bloc. Consequently, their exports to the strong blocs will be adversely affected, while their imports from there will remain either at the same level or increase in the course of time. Mexico is fast becoming a serious competitor to India in textile exports to NAFTA. This effect will be much more profound after the Multi-Fibre Agreement is totally phased out in 2005.

The South Asian region seems to have realised the importance of RTBs very late. This region comprises the developing and least developed countries, which have so far remained more interested in the trivial political and territorial issues rather than the important economic ones. It was not until 1995 that the SAPTA- SAARC Preferential Trade Agreement came into force. As of December 2000, three rounds of negotiations have taken place, under which a total 5553 items at 6-digit level have been listed for preferential access by all member states. Since India is the largest state of the region, it has offered the maximum tariff lines. The LDCs have been accorded a special care in the SAPTA Agreement in terms of more market access and technical and financial assistance by the relatively advanced countries of the region so as to ensure the equitable benefits of integration to all member states. The fourth round of negotiations is in progress. From the second round onwards, non-tariff barriers (NTBs) were also included in negotiations.

The original plan envisaged the realisation of SAARC Free Trade Area (SAFTA) by 2001. However, looking at the slow progress achieved so far, it does not look feasible. By December 2000, only 5553 items have been included under SAPTA by all member states. India imports a total of around 5063 items at 6-digit level from the world, while it (in spite of having given the maximum number of items) extended preferential access under SAPTA to only 2925 items. Since to realise SAFTA, all items will have to be brought under the preferential regime by all member countries, we are not even half-way through to the goal. Moreover, the tariff concessions will have to be increased up to 100 percent on all commodities by all member countries. As of today, the extent of tariff concessions ranges from 5 to 50 percent in case of non-LDCs and 10 to 100 percent in case of LDCs. However, on most of the commodities, it is below 20 percent. Hence, there is a need to deepen the tariff concessions on items already included under SAPTA along with widening of the commodity coverage. However, in the third round, India deepened the concessions on the items offered in the first and second rounds. Further, the non- tariff barriers, which are very prominent in this region, are required to be withdrawn. Pakistan has not yet granted the MFN-status to India. However, NTBs have been included for negotiations from the second round onwards, and India has unilaterally withdrawn all NTBs regarding quantitative restrictions within SAPTA in 1998. Thus, the goal of establishing SAFTA remains an elusive and distant dream.

Group of Eminent Persons (GEP) constituted by the Ninth-SAARC Summit recommended the establishment of South Asian Economic Union (SAEU) by the year 2020 in successive stages. In the first stage, SAFTA is to be created by 2010. In the second and third stages, South Asian Custom Union (SACU) and South Asian Economic Union (SAEU) will be established respectively by the years 2015 and 2020. It also emphasized the special care of the LDCs while going through the regional economic integration process.

As far as the impact of three rounds of negotiations on the trade creation is concerned, the trade turnover within SAPTA has increased from $1435 million in 1994-95 to $1937 million in 1997-98, $2567 million in 1998-99 and to $2046 million in the first three quarters of 1999-2000. In terms of the percentage of the region's total global exports, it increased from 3.8 percent in 1994-95 to 4.8 percent in 1998-99 and 4.9 percent in 1999-2000. Although the trade has increased within the SAARC nations after the implementation of the SAPTA (I), SAPTA (II) and SAPTA (III) rounds of negotiations, the total trade turnover is still much lower in comparison to other regional blocs of the world, like EU, NAFTA, etc. There is lack of complementarities among the SAARC nations. To enhance the complementarities, a conscious attempt should be made by the relatively developed economies by assisting the less developed economies of the region in developing their export capacities. Joint ventures backed by buy-back arrangement can be established not only in LDCs but in other countries of the region as well. FDI should be invited from outside the bloc in areas involving advanced technologies by all the states of the region. An attempt should be made by India to establish the Special Economic Zones (SEZs) on the borders with Nepal, Bangladesh, Pakistan and Bhutan. Border trade, which has not been included in the SAPTA Agreement, should also be brought in its ambit.

Bibliography

Abul Kalam. "SAARC: Sub-regionalism and Bangladesh foreign policy." *Regional Studies*, 15(4) (Autumn19 97): 3-21.

Abdus , Salem sheikh. "Informatisation: The SAARC Scenario." *BIISS Journal,* 19(3), 1998(July):355-65.

Alam, Mohammad Sanzeer and Biswas, Tapash. " Demographic profile of SAARC region." *Regional Studies,*18(3),2000(Summer):148-53.

Anul, Kalam. "Sub-regional cooperation in ASWAN and role of private sector: Relevance for SAARC." BIISS Journal, 20(3), 1999 (july):271-345.

Aggarwal, Bina (994). *A Field of One's Own: Gender and Land Rights in South Asia.* Cambridge: Cambridge University Press.

__________ 1994. "Gender and Command over property: A Critical Gap in Economic Analysis and Policy in South Asia." *World Development* 22 (10), October.

Alam, Mohd Khurshed. "Regional Maritime Cooperation under the auspices of South Asian Association for Regional cooperation (SAARC)." BIISS Journal, 18 (1)(1197): 17-20.

Alatas, Ali. " ASEAN and SAARC: The imperatives of cooperation." BIISS Journal, 19(2)(April 98): 236-44.

APCTT (Asia-Pacific Centre for Transfer of Technology). 1995.*Report on Technology* Promotion *Experience of Selected Asian Countries*. New Delhi.

Associates, L.B. (1998), 'Trade and Investment Opportunities in Sri Lanka,' in 50 Years: In Commemoration of the 50th Anniversary of Independence of Sri Lanka *(Focus: Sri Lanka-Sri Lanka & India-Sri Lanka & SAARC)*. New Delhi.

ADB (Asian Development Bank). 1988.*Foreign Direct Investment in the Asian and Pacific Region*.Manila.

__________ 1994. *Women in Development: Issues, Challenges and Strategies in Asia and the Pacific*.Manila.

__________ 1995. *Breakthroughs in Forestry Development: Experience of the Asian Development Bank*.Manila.

__________ Various Years. *Key Indicators of Developing Asian and Pacific Countries*. Manila.

__________ 1998.*Asian Development Outlook*.Manila.

Baldwin, Peter (1997). 'Planning for ASEAN'. *The Economist Intelligence Unit*. Hong Kong.

Bangladesh. 1994. *Country Paper on the Advancement of Women in the Next Century: Equality, Development and Peace*.Draft Report.

Bashar, Amanullah (1998). 'Post Budget Implications'. *Pakistan and Gulf Economist*. June 22, 29, Karachi.

Bhagwati, J.N. (1978). 'The Anatomy and Consequences of Exchange Control Regimes'. *Studies in International Economic Relations. National Bureau of Economic Research*. New York.

Bhargava , K K.*SAARC and European Union: Learning and Cooperation Opportunities*. (New Delhi: Har- Anand Publications, 1994).

Bhargava , K K. "India ,SAARC and the United States, *Mainstream,* 36(20)(May9, 1998):11-13.

Bhardwaj, R C. "First conference of the association of SAARC speakers and parliamentarians: An overview." *Journal of Parliamentary Information,* 41(3),1995(Sep.):234-46.

Bhalla, A and Bhalla , P. " ASEAN and SAARC." *RIS Digest.* 13 (2-4) (Dec.96):55-90.

Bhattacharya, Basabi and Sutanu Bhattacharya.1992. "South-South Cooperation in Technology: A Sub-regional approach in SAARC Perspective." In Devendra Kumar Das (ed): SAARC: *Regional Co-operation and Development*. New Delhi: Deep and Deep Publication.

Bhattarai, R.B. 1988. "Foreign Direct Investment in Nepal." In *Foreign Direct Investment in the Asian and Pacific Region*. ADB, Manila.

Bhide, S. Kalirajan, K.P. and R.T. Shand (1998). 'India's Agricultural Dynamics: The Weak Link in Development'. *Economic and Political Weekly*. Sep 16, P.A118-A127.

Bhowmik, Debesh. " Monetary Cooperation of SAARC: A Plan for a single Currency." *Southern Economist*, 36(2)(15 May 1997):17-20

Bhutan. 1995. *National Report for the Fourth Conference on Women*. Country Paper.

Blackhurst, Richard, Alice Enders, and Joseph F. Francois, (1995), "The Uruguay Round and Market Access: Opportunities and Challenges for Developing Countries" in *The Uruguay Round and the Developing Economies* (ed.) Will Martin and L. Alan Winters, World Bank Discussion Papers No.307.

Board of Investment (1994), 'Bangladesh: A New Horizon for Investment', Prime Minister's Office, Dhaka.

Board of Investment (1996), 'Sri Lanka Investment Policy and Incentives', Sri Lanka: 21,1620.

Carr, Marilyn et.al. (eds.). 1998. *Speaking Out- Women's Economic Empowerment in South Asia*. New Delhi: Vistaar.

Centre for Policy Dialogue. 1995. Experiences with Economic Reform: *A Review of Bangladesh's Development*. Dhaka.

Chamarik, Saneh and Susantha Goonatilake. 1994. *Technological Independence – The Asian Experience*. United Nations University.

Chakravartty, Sumit. " Pakistan and postponement of SAARC summit." *Mainstream*,37(48),1999(20Nov.):29-30.

Chatterjee, Meera. 1995. "A Gender Perspective on Health Developments: From 1975 to the Future." *The Administrator* 40 (3), July-September.

Chaturvedi, Sachin. 1997. "Bio-safety Policy and Implications in India." *Biotechnology and Development Monitor* No.30, March.

Cherunilam, francis.1998. "International Business Environment". *International Business*. Wheller Publishing. New Delhi.

Chowdhury, Tawfiq. 1988. "Foreign Direct Investment in Bangladesh." In *Foreign Direct Investment in the Asian and Pacific Region.* ADB, Manila.

Choudhary, A R. "SAARC and other regional trade agreements". *Journal of Peace Studies*. 8(3),2001(May-June). 65-68.

Cline, William (1990). *The Future of World Trade in Textiles and Apparel.* Institute for International Economics. Washington.

CPCB. 1997. *Eco-Mark*. Central Pollution Control Board, New Delhi.

Dar, Mueen Ud-Din.1991. "The Role of Foreign Direct Investment in Pakistan's Development." Paper presented at APOIEDP (RSI) Seminar, Seoul.

Das, Ram Upendra. 1997. "Regional Cumulation Provision under European Union's Generalised System of Preferences Scheme: Implications for the SAARC." Paper prepared for the Ministry of Commerce, Government of India. RIS. New Delhi.

Das, S.K. and A. Barua (1996). Regional Inequalities, Economic Growth and Liberalization: A Study of the Indian Economy. *Journal of Development Studies*. Vol. 32(3), pp.364-390.

Datta Roy Choudhry, U. (1993). *Inter-State Variations in Economic Development and Standard of Living.* National Institute of Public Finance and Policy. New Delhi.

Dattatreyulu M. and R.K. Wadhwa. 1993. *Biotechnology Investment Opportunities for India.* Biotech Consortium India Limited. New Delhi.

Dawn (1997), November 22: Karachi.

Debroy, Bibek. "Collective Calling : SAARC Needs to prepare for the agenda of the millennium round." *HIMAL,* 13(9), 2000 (Sep.): 24-28.

Debroy, Bibek. "Intra _regional trade in the SAARC region." *Foreign Trade Review,*23(4)(Jan-Mar89):398-422.

Dubey, Muchkund.1996. *An unequal Treaty: World Trading Order After GATT.* New Age International Publisher. New Delhi.

Debroy, Bibek. 1996. Beyond *the Uruguay Round: The Indian Perspective on GATT.* Response Book. New Delhi.

Dixit, Aabha. SAARC: "Towards Greater Cooperation." *Strategic Analysis.*20(4)(July 97):561-83.

Dubey, Muchkund . "Islamabad's propaganda exercise in Colombo" Mainstream, 36 (33) (Aug.8, 1998):3-5.

Dubey, A K and Tyagi, Ajay. "Involvement of Community in Rural Development : Experience in SAARC countries." *Indian Journal of Social Work,* 57(3) (July 96): 420-41.

Ebdon, Rosamund. 1995. "NGO Expansion and the Fight to Reach the Poor: Gender Implications of NGO Scaling up in Bangladesh." *IDS Bulletin* 26(3), July.

EPW Research Foundation (1997). *National Accounts Statistics of India.* 1950-51 to 1995-96, Revised Edition, Mumbai.

ESCAP (Economic and Social Commission for Asia and Pacific). 1998.*Economic and Social Survey of Asia and Pacific.* Bangkok.

European Commission. 1977. *European Union News.* Newsletter of Delegation of European commission in India. 8, No.4, October-December.

Executive Summary and Recommendations of the Report of Eminent Persons (GEP) prepared by the Group of Eminent Persons constituted by SAARC Committee.

Farid, Shah M. 1993. "Economic Reforms, Poverty and Social Saftey Nets in Social Dimensions of Economic Reforms in Bangladesh." Proceedings of the National Tripartite Workshop, Dhaka, Bangladesh, 18-20, May.

Francois, Joseph F., Bradley McDonald, and Hakan Nordstrom, (1995), "Assessing the Uruguay Round" in *The Uruguay Round and the Developing Economies* (ed.) Will Martin and L. Alan Winters, World Bank Discussion Papers No. 307.

Farooqi, T.Z. 1988. "Foreign Direct Investment in Pakistan." In *Foreign Direct Investment in the Asian and Pacific Region*. ADB. Manila.

GATT, (1994). *Report on Market Access Resulting From the Uruguay Round Multilateral Trade Negotiations.*

Gaan, Narottam. " Comprehensive security for South Asia: An environmental approach." *BIISS Journal*, 20(2), 1999 (April): 103-14.

Ghosh, Buddhadeb and DE, Prabir. " Infrastructure, economic growth and trade in SAARC." *BISS Journal*, 21 (2), 2000 (Aprial):142-74.

Globeerman, Steven. 1994. "The Economics of NAFTA". In Alan M. Rugman (ed.). *Foreign Investment and NAFTA*. University of South Carolina Press. Columbia. PP.3-26.

Goto, Junchi (1988), *Effects of the Multi- fibre Arrangements on Developing Countries: A Survey*, World Bank Staff Working Paper No.102.

Government of Pakistan (1996), 'Why Invest in Pakistan', *Board of Investment*, Islamabad.

Government of Pakistan, *Pakistan's Foreign Trade, Key Indicators: 1997-98*, Ministry of Commerce, Islamabad.

Government of Pakistan. *Economic Survey: 1998-99.* Finance Division, Ministry of Finance, Islamabad.

GOI (Government of India). 1992. *Eighth Five Year Plan 1992-97.*Planning Commission, New Delhi.

__________ 1995.*India.* Ministry of Information and Broadcasting, New Delhi.

__________ 1995. *SIA Newsletter*. Ministry of Industry. May.

__________ 1997. *Agenda Notes for the Conference of SAARC Environment Ministers*. Ministry of Environment and Forests, New Delhi.

Gumminghan and Brendam Barker. 1992. *World Technology Policies, Longman Guide to World Science and Technology*. London: Longman.

Haidari, Iqbal (1997), 'Power Generation', *Economic Review*, May, Pakistan.

Haider, Saraswati. 1996. "Misconceptualized National Policy for Women." *Mainstream* June 22.

Harshe , Rajan. " South Asian Regional Cooperation: Problems and Prospects." *Economic and Political Weekly*,34(19), 199998-14 May):1100-05.

Haq, Mahbub ul. 1996. "Human Development Paradigm for South Asia."*Mainstream.* February, 24.

Hashemi, Syed M. and others. 1996. "Rural Credit Programs and Women's Empowerment in Bangladesh". *World Development* 24(4).

Hasan, M. Aynul. "Conceptual Framework for Growth Triangles". *Pakistan Development Review*,38(4), 1999(Winter): 805-22.

Hindustan Times (1998), May 2, Delhi.

Hirschman, A.O. (1961), *Strategy of Economic Development*, Yale University Press, New Haven.

HM Government of Nepal. 1992. *Nepal: Foreign Investment Opportunities*. Ministry of Industry, Katmandu.

HMGN (1995), 'Industrial Policy 1992', *Nepal Industrial Development Corporation*, Katmandu.

HMGN (1996), 'Procedural Manual for Foreign Investment in Nepal', Ministry of Industry, July, Katmandu.

Islam, Mohammad Jahirul. " Technical cooperation among SAARC countries: problems and prospcts." *BIISS Journal,* 17(1), 1996 (Jan):96-121.

IMF (International Monetary Fund). 1998. *International Financial Statistics.*

Washington.

__________ Direction of Trade Statistics (yearbook and Quarterly), Various issues.

__________ 1998. World Economic Outlook. Washington, D.C.

India Investment Centre (IIC). (1998). *Summary of Joint Ventures and Wholly owned Subsidiaries Abroad.* New Delhi.

Joy, P. A. *SAARC Trade and Development*(New Delhi: Deep & Deep Publications, 1995).

Jackson, Stephen. 1992. "Mainstreaming WID: A Survey of Approaches to Women in Development". *Trocaire Development Review.*

Joshi C.B. 1995. "A Brief Review on the Present Status of Some Technological Sectors in Nepal." Paper presented at a seminar on Technology and Resources Transfer among SAARC Member States, New Delhi, 16-19 May.

Josse. M R. "Bloc within a bloc? A Katmandu Perspective." *Regional Studies,* 15(3)(Summar1997):41-51.

Kalim Bahadur. "Politics of SAARC". World Focus, 22(7), 2001 (July): 7-9.

Kanungo, Rajashree. " United States' trade relations with SAARC countries ." *Journal of Peace Studies*, 5(5), 1998(Sep-Oct):62-69.

Kantawala , Bhavana S. "Inter-and intra- industry international trade among SAARC countries" *Foreign Trade Review*, 32(1-2)(April-Sep. 97):29-72.

Kelegama, Saman (1998), 'Indo-Sri Lanka Economic Relations: Trends and Outlook', in L.B. Associates (ed.): *Sri Lanka 50 Years: In Commemoration of the 50th Anniversary of Independence of Sri Lanka.*

Khan, Ashfaque and Yun- Hwan Kim (1998), 'Pakistan: Foreign Direct Investment and Policy Challenges', Asian Development Bank, Manila.

Khan Mohd Asif Ali and Khan, A Q. " Global investment opportunities and trade in developing economies: A focus on ASEAN and SAARC." *India Quarterly,* 55(1-2), 1999(Jan.-June): 19-59.

Kim Linsu and Carl J. Dahlman. 1992. "Technology Policy for Industrialization : An Integrative Framework and Korea's Experience". *Research Policy* 21.

Kulassoviga S.A. 1992. "Agricultural Biotechnology in Sri Lanka". Paper Presented at ANSAB Meeting at Katmandu.

Kodikara, Shelton U. " Political Dimensions of SAARC." *South Asia Journal.*, 2(1) (Apr-Jun 89):349-71.

Kumar, Nagesh. 1987. "Technology Policy in India: An Overview of its Evolution and an Assessment." In P.R. Brahamananda and V.R. Panchamukhi (eds.): *The Development Process of the Indian Economy*. Bombay: Himalaya. PP 461-492.

Kumar, Nagesh (1992). *Single European Market, Multinationals and Industrial Reorganization.* Occasional Paper No.37, RIS, New Delhi.

Kumar, Nagesh (1994), "Regional Trading Blocs, Industrial Reorganization and Foreign Direct Investment: The case of Single European Market," *World Competition*, vol.18, No.2, December 1994.

Kumar, Nagesh and N.S. Siddharthan. 1997. *Technology, Market Structure and Internationalization*. Chapter 2, Routledge, London.

Kumar, Naresh, et.al. 1998. *Globalization, Foreign Direct Investment and Technology Transfers: Impact on and Prospects for Developing Countries*. London and New York: Routledge.

Kumar, Nagesh (1999), "Competition Policy", *The Economic Times*, 1 September 1999.

Kumar, Nagesh (2000), *Globalization and the Quality of Foreign Direct Investment*.

Lama, Mahendra P. and Prabhakar J. Lavakare. 1996. "Technology Missions for South Asia: Cooperation in High Tech Domain." Paper submitted at SAARC Meeting of the Group of Experts for the Study on Issues of Economic Cooperation. New Delhi. RIS. June 6-7.

Lama, Mahendra P. (1999a), "Integrated Programme of Action in SAARC: Genesis, Evaluation, Constraints and Rationale for Revamping", RIS Occasional Paper.

Lama, Mahendra P. (1999b), 'Energy Cooperation in South Asia: Issues, Challenges and Potentials', Occasional Paper South Solidarity, New Delhi.

Lama, Mahendra P. "SAARC: The Future Ahead." *World Focus*. 22(7),2001(July):14-17.

Lama, Mahendra P. "SAARC: Shallow Regionalism, Political Abstinence and Economic Advocacy." *BIISS Journal*, 21(1), 2000 (Jan.):1-35.

Low, P. (ed.) 1992. International Trade and the Environment. World Bank Discussion Paper No. 159. World Bank. Washington DC.

Mahadeve, B. 1988. "Foreign Direct Investment in Sri Lanka." In *Foreign Direct*

Investment in the Asian and Pacific Region, ADB, Manila.

Mahajan, V.S. (1995). "Structural Reforms and Employment Opportunities with Special Reference to Women." *Political Economy Journal of India* 4 (182) Jan-Jun.

Maskay, Nephil Matangi. "Note on a single currency for SAARC." *Indian Economic Journal*, 46(1) (July -Sep. 98-99): 118-21.

Mathur, A. (1983). Regional Development and Income Disparities in India: A Sectoral Analysis, *Economic Development and Cultural Change.* Vol. 31(3), p.475-505.

Mathur, A. (1987). Why Growth Rates Differ Within India: An Alternative Approach. *Journal of Development Studies.* Vol. 23(2), p. 167-199.

Mc Neely, J.A. 1993. *Parks for Life: Report of the Fourth World Congress on National Parks and Protected Areas.* IUCN, Gland.

Ministry of Commerce and FICCI. *National Schedule of Concessions: First and Second Round of SAPTA*. New Delhi.

Mishra, Pramod K. "South-South Cooperation and SAARC." *Monthly Public Opinion Surveys,* 34(10-11)(Jul/Aug 89): 9-15.

Mishra, Pramod K. "Dhaka to New Delhi: One decade of SAARC." *India Quarterly,* 52(1-2), Jan-June 96: 73-86.

Mohanty, Manoranjan. " Borderless SAARC: A distant dream?." *Mainstream,* 35(260,7june97:9-14.

Mukherji, I.N. (1996), 'South Asian Preferential Trading Arrangement: Assessing Trade Flows in the First Round of Trade Negotiations', Friedrich-Naumann Stiftung, New Delhi.

(1998), 'The South Asian Preferential Trading Arrangement: Identifying Products in India's Regional Trade', *Asia-Pacific Development Journal,* Vol.5, No.1, June 1998.

Mukherji, I.N. "Economic Advantages of SAARC." *World Focus*,22(7),2001(July):10-13.

Muni, S.D. *A Changing Relationship*.(New Delhi: Konark Publishers Pvt. Ltd.,1992).

Muni, S.D. *Pangs of Proximity: India and Sri Lanka's Ethnic Crisis* (New Delhi: Sage Publications , 1993).

Muni, S.D. *Understanding South Asia: Essays in the memory of late Professor (Mrs) Urmila Phadnis*/ edited by S.D. Muni (New Delhi : South Asian Publishers, 1994).

Muni, S D. "SAARC at Crossroads." *HIMAL,* 10(13) (May-June 97): 26-28.

Muni, S D. "SAARC at Crossroads." *World Focus,* 17(7), July 93: 3-5.

Muni, S D. "SAARC: Confidence building exercise." *World focus*, 10(9), Sep. 89:19-22.

Murthy, Padmaja. "Role of Smaller members in the SAARC forum." *Strategic Analysis*, 22(8) (Nov. 98):1179-91

Murthy, Padmaja. " Relevance of SAARC." *Strategic Analysis*, 23(10), 2000 (Jan.):1781-96.

Murthy, Padmaja. " Pakistan and SAARC." *Strategic Analysis*, 22(10), 1999 (Jan):1537-60.

Myrdal, G. (1958). *Economic Theory and Underdeveloped Regions.* . Vora, Bombay.

Nair, K.R.G. (1983). *Regional Experience in a Developing Economy*. John Wiley and Sons. New York.

Nayar, Kuldip. " Musings: Male Summit, Gujaral – Sharif Talks and SAARC. *Mainstream*, 35(24)(24May 1997):5-6.

Panchamukhi, V.R. *et.al.* 1990. *Economic Cooperation in the SAARC Region-Potential, Constraints and Policies*. RIS. New Delhi.

__________ 1994. "India." In Saneh Chamarik and Susantha Goonatilake (eds.): *Technological Independence, The Asian Experience*. United Nations.

Panchamukhi, V.R. 1995. "Economic Cooperation in South Asia: The Crisis of Perceptions." *In Emerging South-Asian Order: Hopes and Concerns*. Media South Asia.

__________ 1995. "Cooperation in South Asia." *Financial Express*, October 11. New Delhi.

Panchamukhi, V.R. and Ram Upendra Das. 1997. "Sub-regional Development in SAARC: Co-operation is the key". *Business Line* (The Hindu) April 4. New Delhi.

__________ 1997. "SAARC Investment Area: Making it a viable proposition."

Business Line (The Hindu) September 30. New Delhi.

__________ 1998. "Rules of Origin under SAPTA." Paper prepared for the Ministry of Commerce, Government of India. RIS. New Delhi.

__________ 1998. "Recent Economic Reforms, Regional Integration and Labour Markets in the SAARC Region." Study conducted for International Labour Organization-SAAT. RIS. New Delhi.

Pandey, Saroj. 1996. "Curriculum and Gender Question: The Indian Experience." *Social Action* 46, July-September.

Quibria, M.G. 1993. ADB Economic Staff Paper No.51. Manila.

Rahman, A. (ed.). 1990. *Science and Technologies in India, Pakistan, Bangladesh and Sri Lanka*. London: Longman.

__________ 1995. *Science, Technology and Development* (Volume 1). Delhi: New Age International Publishers Limited.

Rao, R.A. (1985), 'India's Opportunity for Regional Cooperation in Technology Transfer Among South Countries', Anthology of Papers read out in various seminars on SAARC. SAARC Directorate, Ministry of Foreign Affairs, Bangladesh.

Rao, R.A. (1995), 'Technologies Available for Transfer in SAARC Member States', SAARC Documentation Centre, Delhi.

Rao. V.L., Srinath Baruah, Ram Upendra Das. 1997. *India's Border Trade with Select Neighbouring Countries*. RIS. New Delhi.

Rao, M.G., Kalirajan, K.P. and R.T. Shand (1999), "Convergence of Income Across Indian States: A Divergent View", *Economic and Political Weekly*. Vol. 34,p.769-78.

Ram, A N. " SAARC: Missed Opportunities". *World Focus*, 21(10-12), 2000(Oct.-Dec.) :23-27.

Reed , Ananya Mukherjee. " Regionalization in South Asia : Theory and Practices." *Pacific Affairs,* 70(2)(Summer 1997):233-51.

Regmi Prasad Govind. 1994. *Industrial Growth in Nepal-A Sectoral and Regional Analysis*. New Delhi: Oxford and IBH Publishing Company.

Rey, Sergio J. and D. Montouri (1999). "US Regional Income Convergence: A Spatial Econometric Perspective. *Regional Studies*. Vol. 33(2) p.143-56.

Roy Burman, B K. "Human rights in SAARC countries in perspectives." Mainstream, 37(26), 1999(19 June): 17-19.

Sengupta, Nitish and Banik, Arindam. " Regional Trade and Investment : Case of SAARC." *Economic and Political Weekly*, 32(46) (15-21 Nov. 97):2930-31.

Shahed, Kalam. " SAARC in the context of the nuclearisation of South Asia ." *BIISS Papers*, 17, 1998 (Dec.): 58-81.

RIS (1998/99). *SAARC Survey of Development and Cooperation, 1998/99,Research & Information System for the Non-Aligned and Other Developing Countries*. New Delhi.

SAARC: Regional Cooperation and Development ; Perspectives Problems and Policies/ edited by Debendra Kumar Das and Foreword by V.R. Panchamukhi.(New Delhi: Deep & Deep Publications, 1992).

SAARC: Dynamics of Regional Cooperation in South Asia/ edited by B.C. Upreti.(New Delhi: Kalinga Publications, 2000).

Research and Information System for the Non-Aligned and Other Developing Countries (RIS). 1998. SAARC Expert Group on SAARC Tripartite Study. *SAARC Partnership in Progress: A Visionary Agenda.* New Delhi.

__________ 1998. *Sustainable Use of Bio-diversity: An Agenda for Urgent Initiatives-A Memorandum to the Non-Aligned Movement and G.77.* New Delhi.

"SAARC: Challenges dilemmas." World Focus, 22(7), 2001 (July): 3-24.(Series of articles)

SAARC (South Asian Association for Regional Cooperation) Secretariat.1991. *Study on Trade, Manufactures and Services.* Katmandu.

__________ 1995. *Delhi Declaration Eight SAARC Summit.* New Delhi.2-4 May.

__________ 1996. *SAARC in Brief.* Katmandu.

__________ 1996. *Report of the 14th Meeting of the Technical Committee on Science and Technology.* Katmandu.

__________ 1996. *Report of the 15th Meeting of the Technical Committee on Agriculture.* Katmandu.

__________ 1996. *Report of the 15th Meeting of the Technical Committee on Transport.* Katmandu.

__________ 1997. *Report of the 7th Meeting of the SAARC Technical Committee on Tourism.* Katmandu.

__________ 1997a. *SAARC in Brief.* Katmandu.

__________ 1997b. *Report of the Meeting of the SAARC Environment Ministers.* New Delhi. April 2-3, Katmandu.

__________ 1997. *Report of the 5th Meeting of the Technical Committee on Communications.* April. Katmandu.

__________ 1997. *SAARC Newsletter.* October. Katmandu.

__________ 1997. "Report of the 15th Meeting of the SAARC Technical Committee on Rural Development" and Proceedings of Sixteenth Meeting, as reported in *SAARC Newsletter* October. Katmandu.

__________ 1997. "Proceedings of the 16th Meeting of the Technical Committee on

Agriculture," as reported in *SAARC Newsletter* October. Katmandu.

__________ 1997. "Report of the 1st Meeting of the Technical Committee on

Environment and Meteorology-1996" and the Proceedings of its Second Meeting, as reported in *SAARC Newsletter*, Nov-Dec. Katmandu.

__________ 1998. *SAARC Newsletter.* March-April. Katmandu.

__________ 1998. "Proceedings of the SAARC Information Ministers," as reported in *SAARC Newsletter* May. Katmandu.

__________ *Report of the Third Meeting of Inter-Governmental group on Trade Liberalization to Conclude the Third Round of Trade Negotiations under SAPTA.* Katmandu.

"SAARC Starts to get Serious". *HIMAL,* 10(3) (May-June 97):14-16.

Saxena, Sadhna. 1995. "Education and Women-On the Beijing Agenda." *Economic and Political Weekly* November, 25.

Shand, Ric (1999), (ed.) 'Economic Liberalization in South Asia', Macmillan, Delhi.

Shukla Vijay. " Expectations From SAARC." Third Concept,10(115)(Sep.96):7-10.

Sorsa, P. 1994. *Competitiveness and Environment Standards-Some Exploratory Results.* Policy Research Working Paper 1249, World Bank. Washington, D.C.

Taneja, Nisha. "Informal Trade in SAARC Region." *Economic and Political Weekly,*36(11),2001(17-23 March):959-64.

TERI (Tata Energy Research Institute). 1997. *Growth with Resources Enhancement of Environment and Nature (GREEN-India 2047) –Looking Back to Think Ahead.* New Delhi.

Thant, M., M. Tang and, H. Kakazu. (eds). 1995. *Growth Triangles in Asia: A New Approach to Regional Economic Cooperation.* Asian Development Bank. Manila.

Thapliyal, Sangeeta. " Sub- Regional Cooperation: A Nepalese Perspective for Development" *Strategic Analysis*, 20(1) (April 1997): 163-66.

UN. (United Nations) 1995. Statistical Yearbook. New York.

UNCTAD. (United Nations Conference on Trade and Development). Various years. *World Investment Report.* New York.

UNCTAD (1999), *World Investment Report,* UN, Geneva.

UNDP (United Nations Development Programme). Various years. *Human Development Report.* New York.

UNDP (1999). *Human Development Report.* Oxford University Press. New Delhi.

__________ 1995. *Science and Technology in Bhutan Jan-1993 to July-1994.* Status Report. New York.

UNEP (United Nations Environment Programme). 1997. *Global Environmental*

Outlook 1997. Narobi.

UNESCO (United Nations Educational, Scientific and Cultural Organization). Various years. *Statistical Yearbook.* Paris.

UNIDO (United Nations Industrial Development Organization). Various years. *Industry and Development: Global Report.* New York.

Vyasulu, Vinod. 1993. "New Economic Policy and Technological Change-Towards New Initiatives." *Economic and Political Weekly* July 17-24.

Weerakoon, Dushni. "Does SAFTA have a future?" *Economic and Political Weeky*, 36(34),2001(Aug.25-31):3214-16.

Wignaraja, Poona. 1990. Women, Poverty and Resources. New Delhi: Sage.

World Bank. Various years. *World Development Report.* Washington D.C.

__________ 1998. *World Development Indicators 1998.* Washington D.C.

__________ 1998. *Global Development Finance: Analysis and Summary Tables.* Washington D.C.

__________ 1998. *Global Development Finance: Country Tables.* Washington D.C.

World Conservation Union. 1997. *South Asia Regional Action Plan.* The World Commission on Protected Areas.

Williamson, John. *The Open Economy and The World Economy.* Basics Books, Inc., Publishers. New York.

Williamson, J.G. (1965). "Regional Inequality and the process of National Development: A Description of the Patterns". *Economic Development and Cultural Change.* Vol. 13(4), pp.3-45.

WRI (World Resources Institute). Various years. *World Resources.* Washington D.C.

World Bank (1997). *India: Cotton and Textile Industries – Maximizing the Potential for Growth in a More Competitive Environment.* March 1997.

World Trade Organization (WTO), *Annual Report:* 1997.

http://www.saarcnet.org. National Schedules of Concessions Granted by India.

Index